To Steven Skupski

With the love and
prayers of the members of
St. Philemon's Church, Toxteth,
to mark your Confirmation by
Michael, Bishop of Warrington
at St. Cleopas' Church.
November 28th. 1976.

+ Michael Warrington

MY BELIEF

MY BELIEF

The Faith of an Anglican

Maurice C. Burrell M.A.

MARSHALL, MORGAN & SCOTT
London

MARSHAL, MORGAN & SCOTT, LTD.
BLUNDELL HOUSE
GOODWOOD ROAD
LONDON, S.E.14

ISBN 551 05449 2

MADE AND PRINTED IN GREAT BRITAIN
BY BUTLER AND TANNER LTD, FROME AND LONDON

CONTENTS

To Jill
and for Susan
Timothy and Simon

INTRODUCTION

Ask a Communist, a Mormon or a Jehovah's Witness what he believes, and he will quickly outline the basic doctrines of his movement. Ask a member of the Church of England what he believes and, unless he is exceptional, he will flee to the vicar for help! Of all people who claim to believe something, Anglicans are usually the most ignorant of what it is they are supposed to believe.

There are a number of reasons for this lamentable state of affairs. The most obvious is the large nominal membership of the Church of England. Although about half the population of this country are baptised members of the Church, most of them are Anglicans only in name. Few of them have received any definite Christian instruction. Even among those with a more vital allegiance, there has been little sense of obligation to discover what the Church teaches. While Communists, Mormons and Jehovah's Witnesses spend hours each week learning their doctrines, the average Anglican grumbles if the sermon lasts more than twenty minutes.

This book is intended to be a simple guide to Christian doctrine and practice, understood from an Anglican viewpoint. It is meant to be used as a text-book, and there are questions and suggestions for further reading at the end of the chapters. I have subtitled it 'The Faith of *an* Anglican' for obvious reasons. There are various shades of opinion within the Church of England and, although I am convinced about my own position, I am not so presumptuous as to suggest that this is '*The* Anglican Faith'—pure-bred Anglicanism all through. My own convictions are those of an Evangelical

Anglican, and this is simply my attempt to set out what I believe, and what I think is true Church of England teaching.

I have written especially for Confirmation candidates, though I realise that many of them—the younger ones especially—will need guidance by the leader of their Confirmation course, in studying these pages. Others, such as those looking at Church of England teaching for the first time, or Communicants desiring some kind of 'refresher course', may also find the book useful. It is in two parts—Part 1 seeks to expound the Christian Faith, and in general follows the pattern of the Apostles' Creed; Part 2 is concerned with the Christian Life and discusses Church membership, private Bible reading, prayer, witness and stewardship. But first we must look at Confirmation itself, asking what it is and what it does.

CONFIRMATION

We may use the verb 'to confirm' in two ways; we confirm a statement, a promise or an agreement in the sense of *ratifying* or *endorsing* it. For example, a business man's secretary makes a promise to a customer over the telephone; then, at a later date, he confirms the promise in writing. The other meaning of the verb is to *strengthen*. The two ideas are brought together in Confirmation, where the candidate confirms (ratifies) his baptismal promises and looks to God to confirm (strengthen) him with the Holy Spirit, in whose power alone he will be enabled to keep those promises.

At the time of writing there are two Confirmation services authorised for use in the Church of England—the 1662 Prayer Book service and the Series 2 experimental service. It seems likely that Series 2 or something very much like it will come into general use when the experimental period is over. What follows is written largely with this Series 2 service in mind, though it applies generally to the 1662 service.

The Series 2 service then, begins with prayer which very closely associates Confirmation with Baptism. Readings from the Old and New Testaments follow, and then, sections concerning "The Decision" and "The Profession of Faith". In the first the candidate affirms his allegiance to Christ and his rejection of all that is evil, in the three statements "I turn to Christ", "I repent of my sins" and "I renounce evil". In the second he ratifies the promises made at his baptism, affirming his faith in God the Father who made the world, His Son Jesus Christ who redeemed mankind, and the Holy Spirit who sanctifies the People of God. After further prayer that the Holy Spirit will give the candidate wisdom and understanding, counsel and inward strength, knowledge and true godliness, and holy fear, the Bishop lays his hand upon the candidate's head, saying simply, "Confirm, O Lord, thy servant with the Holy Spirit." The service then concludes with further prayer.

The laying-on of hands is a symbol of blessing found in the Christian Church from its earliest days. Its purpose, according to the post-Confirmation prayer, is to assure candidates of God's favour and goodness towards them. Just as the renewal of baptismal vows emphasises the candidate's part (he must commit himself by confirming the promises), so the laying-on of hands emphasises God's part (the Spirit must empower him if he is to succeed in the Christian life). Confirmation is a reminder, therefore, that we cannot live as Christians in our own strength; we need God's grace, and the act of Confirmation assures us that it is available. It follows of course, that those who are unwilling to be confirmed because, as they say, they "could never keep it up" have missed the whole point of the rite. Being a Christian is not just "me keeping it up"; it is "God holding me up".

PREPARATION FOR CONFIRMATION

The Revised Catechism says, "It is required that persons to be confirmed should have been baptised, be sufficiently instructed in the Christian Faith, be penitent for their sins, and be ready to confess Jesus Christ as Saviour and obey him as Lord." This indicates that there must be both instruction and commitment after Baptism and before Confirmation.

Every candidate is expected to follow a course of pre-Confirmation instruction such as that contained in this book, so that he may gain an intelligent grasp of Christian faith and practice. But a word of warning is necessary: a Confirmation course is not to be regarded as a kind of ecclesiastical eleven-plus! The mere ability to grasp doctrine does not make a person a Christian. Nevertheless, each candidate should do his best to grasp what he can of basic Christianity. He will not understand it all—who does? But as he progresses in the Christian life, things which at present seem difficult may become easier to understand later on.

A Christian, then, is not simply someone who has said 'yes' to a doctrinal creed, but someone who has said 'yes' to Jesus Christ. Personally and decisively, he has committed himself to the Christ of whom that doctrinal creed speaks. The Revised Catechism rightly stresses the importance of this kind of commitment. Candidates must be "penitent for their sins" and "ready to confess Jesus Christ as Saviour and obey him as Lord". This should be kept in mind throughout this book; we shall return to it more than once.

WHAT IS THE AGE FOR CONFIRMATION?

What we have just considered brings us to the question: at what age should people be confirmed? Some say that children should be confirmed before they pass through adolescence. Roman Catholics confirm very young children, but they do not require them to make a public declaration of faith. The Church of England does not specify any age, but in practice the majority are confirmed in early teen-age. No hard and fast rules can be laid down—the age at which children mature physically and mentally varies considerably, and the same is true of spiritual growth. What seems reasonable is the Prayer Book's insistence that candidates should have reached the "years of discretion"; in other words, they must know what they are doing and why they are doing it, and of course they ought to be doing it of their own free-will and not because of any parental or other pressures that may have been brought to bear on them.

There is no disgrace in being confirmed later in life: many people are converted to Christ in middle-age or even later.

They should not fight shy of Confirmation because of the mistaken belief that they are at fault for not having come sooner. Better to be confirmed at fifty and mean it than at fifteen and pretend it.

WHAT FOLLOWS CONFIRMATION?

Confirmation introduces a person to all the privileges and responsibilities of full Church membership. The confirmee becomes a communicant and so has the privilege of partaking of the Sacrament of Christ's Body and Blood. He will be expected to take his full part in the life of the local Christian community, worshipping regularly, giving generously, living consistently, witnessing fearlessly, and serving selflessly. Voluntarily he has signed on in Christ's army. Now he must begin to fight the good fight of faith.

PART 1

CHRISTIAN FAITH

1

BELIEF IN GOD

"I believe in God." The Apostles' Creed, like the Bible, assumes that God exists. It makes no attempt to prove the point. Some people take exception to this attitude. They want to be sure. "Prove to us that God exists", they say, "and we shall listen to everything else you say about Him."

It must be understood that we cannot prove God's existence in a way that is scientifically conclusive. We can prove that a solution is acid by the use of litmus, but we should be foolish if we expect God Almighty to submit Himself to a kind of glorified litmus test! To say that God exists, therefore, is to take a step of faith.

What many people overlook, however, is the fact that it is also an act of faith to say that God does *not* exist! Theism involves the belief in the existence of a God; atheism involves the belief that there is not a God: but both positions are positions of faith. To be a theist or an atheist is, therefore, to be a believer, though the substance of the two faiths differs somewhat! Some would say it requires more faith to be an atheist than to be a theist, but that is another matter.

Although God's existence cannot be proved in a scientifically conclusive manner, there are many indications in the universe that belief in God is not blind belief.

A FIRST CAUSE

Science tells us that everything has its cause, that the law of cause and effect operates in the universe. If this is so, sooner or later we come up against the idea of a First Cause, an 'uncaused cause' from which everything else has originated. Christians believe that this First Cause is God.

A GREAT DESIGNER

What would you think if I were to indicate a painting and tell you that no one painted it? What conclusion would you draw if I were to show you a house and tell you that no one built it? A painting implies an artist; a house implies a builder. In our own experience we have discovered that order and design do not come about by chance. Behind them is a planning and creative mind. If this is true on the level of our everyday human experience (and who would dispute it?), then it seems reasonable to believe that it is true in the universe as a whole. In other words, order and design in the universe suggest that the universe was planned, that behind it there is the directing mind of the Divine Architect.

A MORAL LAWGIVER

Everyone knows there is a difference between right and wrong. We have a means of distinguishing between the two—conscience. Conscience by itself is not infallible; it needs to be educated. People have done all kinds of outrageous things in the name of conscience, and still do. Nevertheless, it remains true that we know there is a difference between right and wrong. From where did this moral sense come? Christians believe it points to the existence of a Perfect Moral Being, to God.

AN OBJECT OF WORSHIP

Belief in some kind of a God is universal. All races at all times have felt the need to worship someone or something. Sometimes this desire to worship has led them into all kinds of strange ways. Uncivilised people have worshipped animals and inanimate objects; civilised people, when they have rejected God as their object of worship, have felt the need to put something in His place. It was a man of profound insight who, misquoting Paul's words, applied them to our age in the form, "Whose god is their *telly*"! Man needs to worship. Christians believe that this basic human need shows that there is a reality which meets it. This reality is God.

I am not claiming for a minute that these four lines of reasoning prove beyond all doubt that God does exist. When you have considered them, and others like them, you will still find that belief in God is an act of faith. But their weight cannot be ignored—if they did nothing more they would certainly indicate that belief in God is far from being belief against one's better judgement.

WHAT IS GOD LIKE?

A patient once told a psychiatrist that he thought God was like the old man in the flat above him who always banged on the ceiling when he made a noise! There are people for whom God is like that—a cantankerous old man, always on the lookout for someone to step out of line.

Others go to the opposite extreme. "He has an old wise face, the most lovest eyes twincling a little, and laughing at our little errers" (*Teenage Religion*, p. 46). Many think of God as a benevolent old Father Christmas, with long white beard and ready smile, who hands out gifts to all and sundry and never bothers how we behave.

There is a certain amount of truth in these ideas—God is holy, and therefore He hates sin; God is love, and therefore He is benevolent: He desires what is best for us. God has shown us what He is like in His Son, Jesus Christ. That is why Jesus said, "He who has seen me, has seen the Father" (John 14:9). But to avoid the error of either extreme, we need to remember that God is both—He is Holy Love.

The Apostles' Creed sums up what Jesus and His followers taught about God, in the words, "God the Father Almighty, Maker of heaven and earth."

GOD THE CREATOR

The Bible states that the universe owes its existence to the creating and sustaining power of God. To put it more simply, God made everything and now continually upholds everything. Later we shall need to consider the relationship between this view and what Science says about the world's origin. For the present it is sufficient to note that the ideas of Divine Creation and of Evolution are not mutually exclusive.

More important for the confirmation candidate is the personal implication of Creation. If God made me, then I belong to Him. If God upholds me, then I depend on Him. If I believe these things, then my whole life ought to be characterised by trust and obedience.

GOD THE ALMIGHTY

Christian thinkers describe God as omniscient, omnipresent, and omnipotent, and this means that God is aware of everything, is present everywhere, and is able to do anything. In short, He knows what He is doing, and He is in complete control.

This raises a problem which we must all face—if God is really like this, why does He allow people to disobey Him, why does He allow the innocent to suffer? Why has He not made us in such a way that we do what He wants without thinking?

God is almighty, so He *could* have made us in such a way that we always obeyed Him without question: when He pulled the strings, we would have performed the correct antics; when He turned on the power, we would have moved as He wished. But let us not delude ourselves into thinking that we should have been human beings, capable of making a voluntary response to Him, able freely to give Him our love and service. We would have been puppets or robots.

In this respect, therefore, God decided to limit His almightiness. He chose to give us freedom. We may choose to believe in Him or reject Him. We may choose to give Him our love and service, or we may choose to withhold both. The responsibility of choice is ours, and with the choice come the consequences. God does not wish it to be otherwise. Would you?

GOD THE FATHER

When we think of the term 'father', we think of personal relationships within the family circle. Ideally, these relationships are always harmonious. Father and children always see eye to eye, there is never any friction between them, they always get on well together. In reality, however, father and children do fall out; the fellowship can be broken. When this happens, a barrier descends between them, and only when they 'make it up' is that barrier removed and fellowship restored. Then we speak of father and children as 'reconciled'.

Jesus taught people to think of God as their Father. He taught His disciples to pray, "Our Father, who art in heaven." Before the coming of Christ, the Jews had occasional glimpses of the Fatherhood of God. When Christ came, He gave the concept new depth and meaning.

The idea is obviously that we should all be true children of our Heavenly Father and that He and we should "get on well together". There should be a perfect harmony between God and us. This ideal relationship hardly ever exists, and the fault is always ours, never His. There is a barrier between God and us, because we are sinners. If we are to be reconciled that barrier must be broken down.

It is the unique claim of Christianity that this barrier is broken down in Christ. We shall consider this in more detail later. For the present, we simply note Christ's claim: "I am the way, the truth, and the life; no one comes to the Father, but by me" (John 14:6).

QUESTIONS

1. Which argument for God's existence do you find most helpful, and why?
2. How would you answer the question, "What is God like?"
3. "If God is almighty, why does He allow wars and suffering?" How would you deal with this problem?

FURTHER READING

Isaiah 40:12–31.
Psalm 139.
Romans 1:18–23.

2

RELIGION AND SCIENCE

"The Bible claims that God made the world in six days. Scientists have proved, however, that God did not make the world. It evolved scientifically." Any teacher will have read statements such as this in a fifth former's essay. There is no doubt that many people still think that science and religion are completely opposed. They believe that no self-respecting scientist can remain a convinced Christian. After the briefest discussion with such people, however, it becomes obvious that most of them have never thought out these opinions. They have not taken the trouble to check the facts to see whether they are as they state them. Perhaps in some cases they are simply using science as an excuse for rejecting Christianity, or at least for not thinking too seriously about Christ's claims.

The idea that a scientist cannot be a Christian is manifestly absurd. The slightest acquaintance with the history of science shows that many of the great scientists of the past were convinced Christians. Dr. Malcolm Dixon has illustrated this in a booklet, *Science and Irreligion,* including in his list such people as Boyle, Kepler, Newton, Faraday, Lister, Simpson and many others.

Turning to the present, if Science and Christianity were incompatible, we should not expect to find scientists in the fellowship of the Christian Church, or Christians employed in important scientific posts. But what are the facts? Some scientists are members of the Church and some churchmen hold important scientific appointments. Professor Charles Coulson is probably the best known British example of a top-rank scientist who is a convinced Christian,[1] but he is far from standing in splendid isolation. There are Christians at all levels of science; there is a body known as the Research Scientists' Christian Fellowship, and its membership is not insignificant. At a more lowly level, in the science department of the school at which I was recently teaching, most of the science teachers were practising Christians, and the one or two who were not would have been the first to admit that it was not their science which kept them from Christ!

I am not claiming that the vast majority of scientists are Christians. All I am saying is that the proportion of scientists who *are* Christians is no smaller than the proportion of Christians in many other walks of life. Some scientists believe, and some do not; just as some journalists, or sportsmen, or engineers, or actresses, or typists, or school-children, believe and some do not. One scientist has written, "There is nothing between the soul of a scientist and Jesus Christ save the disposition of the scientist himself" (*The Christian View of Science and Scripture*, Bernard Ramm, p. 43).

SCIENCE AND THE BIBLE

How then are we to interpret the Bible in general, and Genesis 1–2 in particular? First, it should be noted that the Bible is not a scientific text-book. It is irrational to expect the Bible, the last book of which was completed more than eighteen hundred years ago, to speak in the language of twentieth-century science. In the providence of God the Bible was intended for all peoples of all ages, not just for those trained in accordance with modern scientific method.

Are Genesis 1–2 to be regarded as myth, then? In popular language a myth is an imaginative and untrue story. There are some who like to treat the Bible like this, but such a view does not do justice to the facts. He would be a bold man who would stick his neck out so far as to state that Genesis is merely a fairy-tale.

If the creation story is not a scientific treatise and is not a fairy tale, what is it? It is a record of the origin of things in terms that the simplest may understand. It is in picture language: the author uses poetic symbols. Yet at the same time it is a true record of creation.

This does not mean that we are to think of the six days of creation as six literal days of twenty-four hours each. Nor does it mean that (like some of the sects) we are to date the creation at 4004 B.C. Dr. Ramm maintains, "We have in Genesis 1 a broad, general sketch of creation. To try to prove minute points of geology, biology, botany, or anthropology from it is therefore impossible and should not be attempted" (op. cit., p. 36). On the other hand, he can say that in broad outline geology and Genesis tell the same story.

It remains to consider briefly how evolution fits in with what we have said. The Bible says that the worlds were made by God; science regards them as being formed by natural processes and the action of natural forces. There is no essential disagreement between the two. God created, but why should He not do it through the operation of natural forces in accordance with natural laws? God was the planning Mind behind the whole process.

[1] Note the 'letters' which follow his name: M.A., D.Sc., Ph.D., F.R.S., F.R.S.E.

QUESTION

How would you answer the person who claims, "Science has proved that religion is nonsense"?

FURTHER READING

Science and Irreligion, Malcolm Dixon (Falcon Booklet).
Creation and Evolution, D. C. Spanner (Falcon Book).
Science and Christian Faith, D. M. Mackay (Falcon Booklet).

He said through them comes to us by way of their personalities. Nor does it mean that every part of the Bible is of equal spiritual value—I find more to help me in Romans 5 than in 1 Chronicles 3. But it does mean that the Bible comes from God. This is the answer to our first question, Why is the Bible so important? It is important because behind its human authors is the divine Author, God Himself.

We shall not substantiate that claim in any detail, but there are two lines of thought which may prove helpful.

First, Christ Himself accepted the authority of the Old Testament scriptures. Of this there can be no doubt at all. He did not always accept the way those scriptures were interpreted by the religious leaders of His day, but it was their misinterpretations that He questioned, not the authority of the Old Testament itself. As Dr. J. I. Packer puts it, "The fact we have to face is that Jesus Christ, the Son of God incarnate, who claimed divine authority for all that He did and taught, both confirmed the absolute authority of the Old Testament for others and submitted to it unreservedly Himself" (*Fundamentalism and the Word of God*, p. 55).

The most superficial reading of the Gospels proves this point. Jesus claimed that the whole of His teaching and His life, death and resurrection, were in direct fulfilment of the Old Testament scriptures. Warning His disciples of His coming crucifixion He said, "The scriptures say of the Son of Man that he is to endure great sufferings and to be treated with contempt" (Mark 9:12). He corrected the Sadducean error regarding the resurrection with the words, "You are mistaken, and surely this is the reason: you do not know either the scriptures or the power of God" (Mark 12:24). He stated, "Scripture cannot be set aside" (John 10:35). He told the two on the Emmaus road, "How dull you are! . . . How slow to believe all that the prophets said! Was the Messiah not bound to suffer thus before entering upon his glory?" Then we are told, "He began with Moses and all the prophets, and explained to them the passages which referred to himself in every part of the scriptures" (Luke 24:25–27). Packer sums it up like this, "He ended a life of obedience to Scripture by dying in obedience to Scripture, looking to His Father to raise Him from death in fulfilment of Scripture. Duly He rose; and returned to His disciples to explain to them from Scripture the meaning of what had happened. . . . In life and death, therefore, our Lord devoted Himself to fulfilling the Scriptures" (op. cit., pp. 57f).

Secondly, it should be remembered that the manuscript evidence for the authenticity of the New Testament is better by far than that for other classical writings, the authenticity of which we never question. Professor F. F. Bruce makes this point in *The Books and the Parchments*, and claims that were it not for the response demanded by the New Testament, no one would dream of questioning its authenticity (p. 171).

The Church of England recognises the divine authority of the Bible. It has affirmed that the Bible is the source of true religion (Article VI). It has stated that the Creeds of the Christian Church are accepted only because "they may be proved by most certain warrants of holy Scripture" (Article VIII).

THE BIBLE'S PURPOSE

What is the Bible for? Its main purpose is summed up by Paul: "The sacred writings which are able to instruct you for salvation through faith in Christ Jesus" (2 Timothy 3:15 R.S.V.). The Bible is a book about salvation, and if we wish to know where to find God's salvation we must use this guide-book.

The Bible fulfils this purpose in a number of ways.

First, it shows us what God is like. He is not the benign old gentleman of much popular thought, nor is He the harsh taskmaster waiting for us to step out of line. He is holy love. Therefore he hates sin but offers mercy in Christ to the repentant sinner. Though sin builds a barrier between God and us, in Christ the barrier is broken down and fellowship is restored.

Not only does the Bible show us what God is like; it shows us what we are like. The picture is often very different from the one we paint of ourselves. Like a great spiritual X-ray unit, the Bible shows us what we are really like, not what we appear to be. For this reason it is not always a comfortable thing to read the Bible. We must be ready to face facts, and facts are often very disturbing.

The Old Testament Law plays an important part in showing us what we are like. It does this by proclaiming to us the standard God expects, showing us how far we all fall short of that standard, and pronouncing God's judgement upon transgressors. It has no power in itself either to cleanse us from sin or to make us holy. The Law gives us what R. A. Cole calls in his commentary on *Galatians* (Tyndale Press, pp. 106ff) "an awakened sense of sin" teaching us our "moral bankruptcy". Paul's letter to the Galatians has much to say on this subject, particularly in chapter three. The Apostle says, "Scripture has declared the whole world to be prisoners in subjection to sin, so that faith in Jesus Christ may be the ground on which the promised blessing is given, and given to those who have faith. Before this faith came, we were close prisoners in the custody of law, pending the revelation of faith. Thus the law was a kind of tutor in charge of us until Christ should come [or, to conduct us to Christ], when we should be justified through faith" (Galatians 3:22–25).

Having shown us what God is like and what we are like, the Bible next fulfils its purpose of leading us to salvation by showing us what Christ has done. Its message is essentially the message of the Cross. Through Paul it tells us, "Christ died for us while we were yet sinners, and that is God's own proof of his love towards us" (Romans 5:8). Through Peter it reminds us, "Well you know that it was no perishable stuff, like gold or silver, that bought you freedom from the empty folly of your traditional ways. The price was paid in precious blood, as it were of a lamb without mark or blemish—the blood of Christ" (1 Peter 1:18–19). Again, "In his own person he carried our sins to the gallows, so that we might cease to live for sin and begin to live for righteousness. By his wounds you have been healed. You were straying like sheep, but now you have turned towards the Shepherd and Guardian of your souls" (1 Peter 2:24–25). Through John it tells us that Christ is "the propitiation for our sins" (1 John 2:2).

The Old Testament sacrifices and ceremonies are visual aids, object lessons emphasising the need for someone to come and die to take away our sins. They point forward to Calvary. The New Testament sacraments of Baptism and Holy Communion are a constant reminder of the One who did come and who did die to take away our sin. They point back to Calvary. As we think of the Bible in this way we see that the Cross is the key which unlocks the Bible's treasures.

The Bible takes us a stage further on the road to salvation. Having shown us what Christ has done, it shows us what we must do. It indicates the response to God's love which we must make if we are to benefit from it. God is holy love. We are sinners in need of salvation. Christ came and died to take away our sin. These are the objective facts of the Gospel declared in the Bible. But the Bible does not leave us there. It urges us to claim our share in what Christ has done for everyone. Again, it is Paul who best makes the point. After stating that God "has reconciled us men to himself through Christ", as Christ's ambassador he tells his readers, "In Christ's name, we implore you, be reconciled to God" (2 Corinthians 5:18 and 20).

4

CHRIST'S SONSHIP

"In the beginning God." "I believe in God." These affirmations from the Bible and the Apostles' Creed provide common ground to most religions, for belief in God (or a god or gods of some kind) is universal. Christianity goes much further. As its name implies, it involves something more than belief in God. So the Apostles' Creed continues, "And in Jesus Christ His only Son our Lord." What do Christians believe about Jesus Christ? This and the next eight chapters will attempt to answer that question.

THE NAME 'JESUS'.

'Jesus' was a common enough name when Christianity's Founder was born. It is the Greek equivalent of the Hebrew 'Joshua'. The name means "the Lord's salvation". Therefore, before Christ was born Joseph was instructed to call Him 'Jesus (Saviour)', "For", said the angel, "He will save his people from their sins" (Matthew 1:21 N.E.B.).

The significance of the name is that it spotlights the purpose of Christ's coming. He did not come merely to set a good example, though the world would be a far better place if people followed the example which He set. He did not come merely to teach, though no other teaching can be compared with His. He came pre-eminently to save, and this we acknowledge every time we call Him Jesus. To ignore this fact is to throw away the key to the Bible. If there is no sin from which we need to be saved, the Christian Gospel is much ado about nothing. But we do need to be saved and there is a Saviour, and we are glad to be reminded of both in our Lord's name, Jesus.

THE TITLE 'CHRIST'

We tend to think of the words 'Jesus Christ' as our Lord's forename and surname, rather like John Smith, or Bill Jones. Certainly 'Jesus' is a name (as we have seen), but 'Christ' is properly a title rather than a name. It is the Greek equivalent of the Hebrew 'Messiah'. Used of Jesus it means that He is God's anointed One, the One sent by the Father in fulfilment of the Old Testament Messianic prophecies.

Steeped as they were in the Old Testament scriptures, the Jews had learnt to look forward to the day when God would send His Messiah to deliver His people. This Messiah would be a great leader, an ideal king. By the time of Christ's birth, however, many of them had come to think of this deliverance in political and military terms. The Jewish nation had become part of the Roman Empire, and the Jews expected the Messiah to lift the Roman yoke from their shoulders and to lead them into political independence.

Jesus put an end to these dreams. Although He had certainly come to deliver them, that deliverance was from sin, not from the Romans. He would fulfil His ministry, not by taking over political control with the backing of military power, but by dying on a Roman cross and then by rising from the dead. As He told Pilate at His trial, His kingdom was not of this world.

When people grasped what His teaching involved, most of them no longer wished to follow Him. They had overlooked those Old Testament prophecies pointing to a suffering deliverer. They were even less inclined to follow Jesus when He added, "If anyone wishes to be a follower of mine, he must leave self behind; he must take up his cross and come with me" (Matthew 16:24 N.E.B.).

This is still Christ's way for His disciples. There is a cost to the Christian life. Christ does not promise His followers an easy way. It is good for those preparing for Confirmation to face up to this fact before they commit themselves to follow in the footsteps of Jesus.

THE STATUS 'SON'

All Christians are children of God, but there is a difference between our sonship and that of Jesus Christ. We *become* children of God when we receive Christ in faith (John 1:12). Christ *has always been* THE Son of God in a unique sense. Just as God has always been the Father, so Jesus has always been the Son. That is why we speak of Christ as the *eternal* Son of God. Jesus himself led the way to this description when He said, "Before Abraham was born, I am" (John 8:58).

The Apostles' Creed does little more than stress the uniqueness of Christ's sonship. It describes Him as God's only Son. The other Christian creeds are more specific. Both the Nicene Creed and the Athanasian Creed take great pains to stress that the Son is one with the Father and that He is God in the full sense of that word. They found it necessary to do so because when they were formulated there were heretics (like the Jehovah's Witnesses today) who denied the full diety of Christ and spoke of Him as a kind of secondary god (*a* god, with a small 'g'). At the same time, these creeds followed the New Testament in maintaining that Father and Son are two distinct Persons.

Later we shall consider the relationship between Father, Son and Holy Spirit. All I ask you to do at present is to note carefully that the Christian faith states that Jesus, the Son of God, is *God* in the full sense of that word. As Son of Man He is, at the same time, perfect Man. God became Man in order that we might be saved. He stooped down to lift us up.

QUESTION

What do the following mean, and what do they tell us of what Jesus *is* and what He has *done*: 'Jesus', 'Christ', and 'Son'?

FURTHER READING

Mere Christianity, C. S. Lewis (Fontana), pp. 39–63; 130–156.

5

CHRIST'S LORDSHIP

This book is based very largely on the Apostles' Creed. The word 'creed' comes from the Latin 'credo', meaning 'I believe'. Thus a creed takes its name from the fact that 'I believe' are its opening words. There are three creeds in the Book of Common Prayer. The simplest is the Apostles' Creed, so called not because the apostles compiled it but rather because in substance it is truly apostolic. In its present form it dates from about A.D. 750. The Nicene Creed, used in the Communion Service, dates from the middle of the fifth century, though it enshrines the teaching first set out at the Council of Nicaea in A.D. 325. The longest and most difficult of the creeds, rarely used nowadays in church services, is the Athanasian Creed. It probably originated in Gaul at the beginning of the sixth century.

The earliest of all creeds, however, was the simple statement, "Jesus is Lord". This was the public confession of faith made by converts at their baptism. So we find Paul writing to the Romans, "If on your lips is the confession, 'Jesus is Lord', and in your heart the faith that God raised him from the dead, then you will find salvation" (Romans 10:9). This simple creed is also echoed in Paul's famous passage in Philippians 2, which reaches its climax as Paul looks forward to the day when every tongue would confess that "Jesus Christ is Lord, to the glory of God the Father" (verse 11).

Elsewhere Paul describes Jesus as 'Lord' well over a

hundred times. The other New Testament writers follow his lead. So, from the earliest days of Christianity, 'Lord' was the one word which best summed up all that Christians believed about Jesus Christ. No other word was used with anything like the same frequency. It is not surprising to find, therefore, that all three historic creeds speak of Jesus Christ as Lord.

"I believe . . . in Jesus Christ, His only Son, our Lord" is what we confess every time we join in the Apostles' Creed. It is easy to say this, but what does it mean in terms of faith and works? Many thousands of books have been written in attempts to explain it, and the fact that more are produced each year shows that no author has yet exhausted all its implications. Basically, however, to call Jesus Christ 'Lord' (and mean it!) is to recognise that He is the One to whom we owe absolute allegiance. He is the 'boss': what He says goes.

Christians of the first three centuries A.D. had no doubt that Christ's Lordship meant just that. Successive Roman emperors, intoxicated with a sense of their own importance, issued decrees demanding absolute allegiance from their subjects. Every Roman citizen was expected to recognise that Caesar was a god and to acknowledge the fact by burning incense before his image. Refusal to proclaim that "Caesar is Lord" was regarded as disloyalty, and the punishment was usually death. Christians were placed in an impossible position; their scriptures told them to support those who ruled over them, and to pray for them. But they could not remain faithful to their baptismal profession, "Jesus is Lord", and also obey the emperor's edict and confess that "Caesar is Lord". Many did remain faithful to Christ despite unbelievable tortures and even death.

One of the best examples is Polycarp, veteran bishop of Smyrna in Asia Minor, who was put to death in the middle of the second century A.D. When soldiers arrived to arrest him, he asked them to allow him a further hour of freedom so that he could pray, and he ordered his servants to provide the soldiers with a meal while they waited. Later, as he faced his accusers, he was advised to remember his great age and to deny Christ. His reply is a classic example of Christian steadfastness: "Eighty and six years have I served Him and He never did me no wrong. How shall I blaspheme my King who has saved me?" He was then taken away and executed.

This is not an isolated example. During the first three hundred years of the Church's history, many hundreds of Christians were thrown to the wild beasts, were roasted alive, were burnt at the stake or beaten to death by wild mobs, and usually the accusations against them was that they would not call the emperor 'Lord'.

These early Christians knew that to call someone 'Lord' was to acknowledge their absolute allegiance to him. For them there was only one whom they were willing to acknowledge in this way. Although what we now call the Apostles' Creed was not in existence in their day, they would have been proud to say and mean, "I believe . . . in Jesus Christ, His only son, our Lord".

As twentieth-century Christians, we are not required to swear absolute allegiance to any man or system (though the patriotic hymn "I vow to thee, my country" comes very near to asking us to do it!). It is easy for us to use the words, "Jesus is Lord"; But we must never forget what they involve. Jesus is our King, our Owner, our Master—'boss'! We must worship and obey Him.

QUESTION

"Jesus is Lord." What effect should such a belief have on our lives?

FURTHER READING

Philippians 2:5–11.

Mere Christianity, C. S. Lewis (Fontana), pp. 162–188.

6

CHRIST'S BIRTH

When Christians say the Apostles' Creed, they profess faith in Jesus Christ who "was conceived by the Holy Ghost, Born of the Virgin Mary". They are saying what Christians have believed from the earliest days, that although the *birth* of Jesus Christ was natural in that He was born of a woman in the normal way, His *conception* was supernatural in that He was conceived without a male sperm fertilising the female ovum. Opponents of Christianity have always ridiculed this belief. Some have said it is based on old wives' tales; others have maintained that it was a clumsy attempt to cover up an illegitimate birth. Even some supporters of Christianity (including some Christian leaders) have declared that little is to be gained from seeking to retain a belief which the world at large will not accept. But, as I shall try to show, belief in Christ's birth of a virgin is an integral part of New Testament Christianity.

THE EVIDENCE FOR THE VIRGIN BIRTH

The New Testament contains two independent accounts of the Virgin Birth, Matthew 1:18–25 and Luke 1:26–38. It will help if, before you read the rest of this chapter, you read these two passages.

Matthew's account tells the story from Joseph's point of view. We are told that Joseph thought the worst when he discovered that his fiancée was pregnant. His natural reaction was to break off the engagement (though a Jewish betrothal was much more binding than our engagement). However while he was considering this course of action, he was told in a dream that Mary's conception was supernatural, "It is by the Holy Spirit she has conceived this child." This is stated to be a fulfilment of Isaiah's prophesy, "A virgin shall conceive and bear a son."

Luke's narrative tells the story from Mary's point of view. The Angel Gabriel told her that she was to conceive a son without experiencing sexual intercourse. Despite her understandable surprise, Mary believed the divine messenger, and in due course gave birth to Jesus in the manger at Bethlehem.

One of the first questions people ask is, "Can we rely on these stories?" It is impressive to notice that neither writer attempts to water down the difficulties of the Virgin Birth. Matthew stresses Joseph's fears that his wife-to-be had been unfaithful to him; Luke, the New Testament's most careful historian, describes Mary's surprise and her natural question, "How can this be, since I have no husband?" Neither account reads like the attempt of a prejudiced author to "pull a fast one". On the contrary, they read like a sober recording of facts by writers who are not afraid to tell the whole story. A writer inventing the story could have made a much more convincing job of it by removing all the difficulties. As it is, each is telling the truth as he knows it and so states it plainly, without any attempt to dress it up.

IS A VIRGIN BIRTH POSSIBLE?

"How can this be?" The question Mary asked is one that will concern us all. Is a Virgin Birth possible?—and this really boils down to two other questions, "*Could* God do it?", and "*Would* God do it?."

To the first of these questions, the answer is obvious; if we believe that God exists and that He is almighty (two things which all Christians would maintain), we must allow the possibility. God could do it. It would be possible for Him to cause Jesus to be born of a Virgin.

But *would* he do it? Surely He would not violate His own

natural law in this way? It is important to keep discussion of this point in its right context. God was about to intervene by sending His Son to save mankind. Is it not reasonable to assume that so unique an intervention, involving as it did that God should become Man, would be inaugurated in a unique manner? God was entering His world to deliver it from bondage. In the light of so stupendous a fact the Virgin Birth is quite reasonable.

SOME TECHNICAL TERMS

Sooner or later people who wish to understand the Christian faith have to take the trouble to learn some of the technical terms of Christianity, just as those wishing to learn engineering, or football, or knitting have to learn the technical terms of those occupations. Now is as good a time as any to consider two technical terms of Christianity—*pre-existence* and *incarnation*.

When Christians speak of Christ's pre-existence they are referring to the belief that the life of Jesus Christ did not begin when He was born in a manger in Bethlehem. Before He came into this world, He had existed with His Father in heaven. In fact, Christians go further than this, believing that Jesus Christ has existed eternally with His Father. Hence He is called the eternal Son of God.

What happened in Bethlehem was that He who has always existed as the Son of God in heaven, now took our flesh upon Himself. God became Man. He did not cease to be God, but in addition He became Man. This is what we mean by the incarnation. How did it happen? This is something we cannot begin to understand, but is it reasonable to expect to confine the infinite God in our finite minds? If we could understand everything about God, He would not be God.

QUESTION

Was it necessary for Christ to be born of a virgin?

7

CHRIST'S DEATH

The Apostles' Creed states the historical fact of Christ's death, but it makes no attempt to state what that fact means to us today. It tells us that Jesus Christ "Suffered under Pontius Pilate, Was crucified, dead and buried",[1] but it does not say why Christ died or what benefits come to us as a result. If we wish to discover the meaning of the Cross, we have to go from the Creed back to the New Testament.

THE FACT OF SIN

The New Testament will have nothing to do with the popular belief that man is capable of such self-improvement that eventually, through his own efforts, he will overcome his faults, solve his problems, and establish a kind of heaven on earth. On the contrary, it tells us that man is a sinner both by birth and choice. From birth he has a natural bias towards sin. Just as in the game of bowls the bias of the bowl takes it off to the right or left, so our 'bias' takes us off from God's way into the ways of sin. This means we become in practice what we are by nature—sinners.

THE CONSEQUENCES OF SIN

God is not merely the benevolent old gentleman of much popular thought. He does not, in the teenager's word—laugh at our little errors. He is not one who would never dream of making demands on people, or of punishing them if they fall below standard. God is holy, and this means that He hates sin. Christ made it crystal-clear that God will judge and punish eternally the unrepentant sinner. People sometimes say that whereas the Old Testament speaks of a God of wrath, the New Testament speaks only of a God of love, but anyone who takes the trouble to read the Bible will soon discover that this is not true to the facts. Both Testaments show that God takes a serious view of sin. The New Testament goes on to show that it was precisely because of His serious view of sin that God sent His Son to take it away. Christ did not come merely to be the world's example, but to be the world's Saviour. We have only ourselves to blame if we spurn salvation and face judgement.

THE REMEDY FOR SIN

God is holy, but He is holy love. Therefore He has provided the means by which we may be cleansed from sin and reconciled to Himself. This is the way of the Cross. This is why the New Testament is full of the Cross, and cannot be understood apart from the Cross. In the Gospels, for example, the narratives of Christ's death and subsequent resurrection occupy nearly half of St. John's Gospel and about a third of the others. The same emphasis is found throughout the New Testament; the apostolic writers say more about the death of Christ than about anything else. Moreover, they all make it quite clear that Christ's death was not just the tragic end of a wonderful life, but rather part of God's plan for the salvation of the world.

I am not going to pretend that I can fully understand and explain how Christ's death can save us, but there are certain basic ideas which help us to begin to understand what the Cross is all about. They come from the Biblical teachings concerning sacrifice, redemption, and reconciliation.

1. Sacrifice

The New Testament speaks of Christ's death as a sacrifice for sin. The Jews were brought up, in the days prior to Christ, to see the connection between the sacrificial death of an animal and their own forgiveness. These sacrifices were meant to be visual aids, object lessons, to teach the truth in a sacramental way to the spiritually immature. The sacrifices pointed forward to the death of Christ and the blessing of forgiveness that would become available as the result of His death. Just as in the Old Testament these sacrifices pointed forward to Christ's death, so for us the Holy Communion service points back to that death. Neither can be understood unless we see that on the Cross Jesus was offering His sinless life as a sacrifice for the sins of the whole world. John the Baptist summed it all up when he cried, "There is the Lamb of God" (John 1:36).

2. *Redemption*

Redemption reminds us that there is a slavery of sin (Romans 6:17) and a consequential death (Romans 6:23) from which we need to be delivered. Christ, by paying the redemption price, has made it possible for us to be delivered. He Himself said, "The Son of Man did not come to be served but to serve, and to surrender his life as a ransom for many" (Mark 10:45). So the cost of our redemption was the death of Christ on the Cross, and Paul can write, "In Christ our release is secured and our sins are forgiven through the shedding of his blood" (Ephesians 1:7).

3. *Reconciliation*

This New Testament theme reminds us that there is enmity between God and unrepentant sinners. There is a barrier between the Holy God and us, a barrier which is of our making. When Christ died on the Cross, He pierced the barrier and made it possible for us, in Him, to have fellowship with our Maker. In Christ we become reconciled to God. There are four important New Testament passages dealing with this theme, Romans 5:10f, 2 Corinthians 5:18ff, Ephesians 2:11ff and Colossians 1:19ff. They would repay careful study. Perhaps the most important verse of them all is 2 Corinthians 5:19, "God was in Christ reconciling the world to himself". This will not allow us to think of Christ's death in the crude terms of an angry and offended God being placated by an independent mediator. God is in the whole plan for our salvation from start to finish.

In dealing with these three themes, I have tried to stress the objective fact of the Cross and its consequences for us. It must be remembered, however, that God does not force His love upon us; Christ does not save us against our will. There is a subjective response which we have to make to Christ. To put it more simply, He died for the sins of the whole world, but we have to claim by faith our share in what He has done for everyone. So St. Paul pleads, 'Be reconciled to God!' (2 Corinthians 5:20).

[1] CHRIST'S DESCENT INTO HELL

One clause of the Apostles' Creed which has puzzled many is, 'He descended into hell'. The Series 2 Orders of Morning and Evening Prayer clarify its meaning with the footnote, "meaning here, 'the place of the departed' ". The Bible is not explicit about what happens to the human spirit immediately following death, though it does point to the existence of an intermediate state between death and final resurrection. The Greek word for this intermediate state is *Hades* (the equivalent of the Hebrew *Sheol*) and it is Hades to which the Apostles' Creed refers.

As well as the two words above, there is a third word, *Gehenna*, often translated as 'hell' in English. The name 'Gehenna' was drawn originally from the Valley of Hinnom outside Jerusalem. It had become the city's rubbish dump, and because fires were always burning there it became a symbol of eternal punishment. This is the Greek word translated 'hell' in Mark 9:43ff, "If your hand is your undoing, cut it off; it is better for you to enter life maimed than to keep both hands and go to hell and the unquenchable fire. And if it is your foot that leads you astray, cut it off; it is better to enter life a cripple than to keep both your feet and be thrown into hell."

QUESTIONS

1. What did Jesus achieve by His death?
2. How do the Sacraments of Baptism and Holy Communion remind us of Christ's death?

FURTHER READING

Romans 5:6–11.
1 Corinthians 1:18–2:5.
The Meaning of the Cross, F. Colquhoun (I.V.F.)
Journey into Life, N. Warren (Falcon Booklet).

8

CHRIST'S RESURRECTION

Without Christ's resurrection, the Christian faith would not exist. There might be a religious sect made up of people trying to follow the teaching of a man called Jesus who gave his life in an attempt to further his views, but this would not be New Testament Christianity. The Christian faith is essentially faith in a Person, Jesus Christ, Who is both God and Man, who was sent into this world by His Father in order to give His life to save us, and who rose victoriously over the worst that evil could do to Him. Therefore Christians will agree with J. S. Whale's words: "Belief in the Resurrection is not an appendage to the Christian faith; it is the Christian faith. . . . It is not tacked on to the Gospel story to make a happy ending, or to hide what without it would be the supreme tragedy of history; it is implicit in the story from the beginning" (*Christian Doctrine,* p. 69). So the Apostles' Creed affirms triumphantly, "The third day He rose again from the dead."

THE EVIDENCE FOR THE RESURRECTION

Opponents of Christianity are quick to decry the resurrection, but many of them never take the trouble to consider the evidence. Before proceeding with this chapter, read Matthew 27:51 to 28:1–20; Mark 15:40 to 16:1–8, Luke 24, and John 20–21. Now consider the evidence.

Christ's Resurrection

1. *The Empty Tomb*

All the Gospel writers affirm that the grave was empty. Various attempts have been made to explain away the significance of this fact.

It has been maintained by some that Jesus did not really die at all. His sufferings caused Him to fall into a deep coma which His executioners mistook for death. He was put into the tomb in this unconscious state but later revived and escaped. His disciples believed (quite wrongly) that He had risen from the dead.

To hold such a theory involves believing that someone who had been scourged and crucified, who had hung in the blazing sun for hours and had a spear thrust into His side, would have survived such treatment. This in itself is not impossible as we know from medical case histories today, though it should be remembered that modern 'miraculous recoveries' usually take place under expert medical care and hospital treatment. But much more is involved in the case of Jesus. We are being asked to believe that after undergoing the suffering which brought about this coma He not only revived without any human helper or care at all, but then removed Himself from the graveclothes and the sealed tomb, pushed aside the great stone blocking the entrance, avoided the guards, and presented Himself to His disciples and convinced them that He had risen from the dead. It also involves a belief that Jesus deliberately misled His disciples. Most people agree that such a theory does less than justice to the facts, and it finds few protagonists today.

Others who do not believe in the resurrection argue that the women went to the wrong grave on that first Easter morning and that this accounts for the story of the 'empty tomb'—it was empty because it had never been used. When they found it empty, their imagination did the rest. But look again at the Gospel accounts. After the visit of the women, Peter and John ran to the tomb to see for themselves. Are we to believe they made the same mistake? If they did, are we to assume that they were not put right by Joseph of Aramathea and Nicodemus, the two secret disciples who had buried Jesus in Joseph's tomb?

Others allege the grave was empty because Christ's body had been removed by His disciples. Obviously this theory is more worthy of consideration than the two we have mentioned already, but there is strong evidence against it. The grave was guarded; further, after the crucifixion the disciples were scared of being seen in public, fearing arrest, and thus were hardly likely to take the great risk of stealing His body. Later on these disciples preached publicly about the resurrection and were even prepared to face death rather than to cease their testimony. Is it conceivable that they would have been prepared to die for something which they knew was a lie? Whatever else is to be said about martyrs, it must surely be acknowledged that they suffer for what they believe to be right and true.

Yet others claim that Jesus's enemies removed His body. What motive would they have for this action? It could only have played into the hands of the disciples, whose faith they were trying to stamp out. But if they did remove the body, why did they not produce it as evidence of the fallacy of the Gospel when the apostles began to preach the resurrection in Jerusalem? This would have stamped out Christianity once and for all. The fact that they did not do this is strong evidence that they had no body to produce.

2. *Christ's Appearances*

The New Testament records ten appearances of the Risen Lord. He appeared to His disciples, to the women returning from the sepulchre, to Peter at an undisclosed rendezvous, to the two on the Emmaus Road, to ten disciples in the Upper Room, to these ten and Thomas a week later, to seven disciples fishing on the Sea of Galilee, to others at the Ascension, to Paul on the Road to Damascus, and to more than five hundred Christians on another occasion. Opposition to this evidence falls into two main categories.

Some say the disciples invented the stories, but if you read the accounts carefully you will see that they read like eye-witness stories rather than fairy tales. If the disciples had invented the stories, they would surely have made a better job of it! For instance, there is no description of the actual resurrection, an opportunity too good to missed by a writer of fiction. Again, is it likely that in such a case these narratives would have depicted the apostles as doubting men? But, as we have seen already, the strongest argument against this view also lies in the events that followed, for these same disciples went out and preached the resurrection despite great suffering and even death for doing so.

Others claim the disciples were suffering from hallucinations. The disciples were undoubtedly sincere, but they were sincerely wrong. They believed Jesus had appeared to them but they were 'seeing things'. Now, if only one or two disciples had claimed to see the risen Jesus this theory might be taken seriously, but as we have seen there were at least ten appearances to different groups at different times and places and once over five hundred people were involved. If one child in a class persistently claims to see a mouse in the room against the evidence of the rest, the teacher may justifiably discount the claim; but if the whole class seriously makes the same claim, the teacher would be foolish not to take some notice. In the evidence for the appearances we are not taking account of one or two neurotic people, but with many different people who believed because of what they saw.

3. *Transformed Disciples*

When their Master was arrested, all the disciples forsook Him and fled. Fearing that they might suffer the same fate at the hands of the Jews, they locked themselves in an upper room. Even Peter, the man of rock, who had sworn that come what might he would stand by Christ, had denied that he knew Him when the test came. But, six weeks later, what a transformation! The cowards had become courageous. In the heart of Jerusalem, the headquarters of the priests who had engineered Christ's death, the disciples proclaimed publicly and fearlessly that Jesus was alive.

What had happened to transform them? The obvious

answer is the correct one. What they were saying was true. They *had* seen Jesus. He *was* alive. Christ had triumphed over death. That being so, there was no need for them to fear anything that their enemies could do.

We have spent many pages on the evidence for the Resurrection, but I make no apology for this—for if Jesus was not raised Christianity is meaningless. But He was raised. The Resurrection is a fact rooted in history. But the Christian Gospel will not let us rest content with the intellectual acceptance of this fact. We must consider, therefore, why Jesus rose, and how His resurrection affects us today.

First, the Resurrection of Christ is a complete vindication of all that He claimed. He said He was the One sent by the Father to save mankind. He stated that those who gave heed to His words and put their trust in the God who sent Him already had hold of eternal life. He taught that He would be killed but three days later would rise from the dead. The fact that He *did* rise completely vindicates these and all His claims.

Secondly, the Resurrection means that those who trust Him are assured of salvation. They possess this assurance, not because of any merit which *they* have earned, but because of what *Christ* has achieved. Their basis of salvation is not what they have done for themselves, but what Christ has done for them.

Thirdly, the Resurrection clearly indicates that death is not the end. The victory that Christ achieved is a victory shared by all whose trust is in Him. We shall have more to say about this in chapters 20 and 21.

Fourthly, the Resurrection assures Christians that Christ is with them all the time. Our object of faith and allegiance is not just a historical figure, but a present, living, victorious Saviour who is with us always.

The Resurrecton means at least all this—and much more besides!

QUESTIONS

1. Is the Resurrection of Christ as important as Christians believe?
2. Discuss the evidence for the Resurrection.

FURTHER READING

Man Alive, Michael Green (I.V.F.).
The Evidence for the Resurrection, J. N. D. Anderson (I.V.F.).
Who Moved the Stone?, F. Morison (Faber).

9

CHRIST'S ASCENSION

The Authorized Version of the Bible contains three accounts of Christ's Ascension: Mark 16:19f, Luke 24:50ff, and Acts 1:9ff. Scholars are now generally agreed that only the Acts passage was part of the original manuscript. This does not mean, however, that the Ascension is built on slender evidence, for other New Testament books show that Peter, Paul, John and the writer to the Hebrews all accept it as historical fact.

How are we to think of the Ascension in this scientific age? As a Sunday School pupil I used to sing with gusto, "There's a Friend for little children above the bright blue sky." Today I would use these words with reservations, for I do not think of heaven as 'up there' in an astronomical sense. We should not be surprised when astronauts fail to locate heaven as a planet in space. But the hymn-writer's theology is better than his astronomy, for the second verse says, "There's a home for little children . . . where Jesus reigns in glory" and succeeding verses outline the blessings which come to us because Jesus thus reigns.

CHRIST THE KING

The Apostles' Creed states that Christ "ascended into heaven, And sitteth on the right hand of God the Father Almighty". This is an important New Testament emphasis. When He became Man, Christ voluntarily laid aside His rights as God. He did not cease to *be* God, but He ceased to be treated as God. On earth He lived a life of complete humility, right from the moment of His birth in a Bethlehem stable to His death on a Roman cross. His life is a perfect example of self-sacrifice. Everything that He endured, He endured voluntarily in order that we might be saved from sin and given new life in Him. His Incarnation and His Crucifixion show us how He stooped down. His Resurrection and His Ascension show us how God raised Him up.

One of the most important New Testament passages dealing with this theme is Philippians 2:5–11. Read it carefully in the New English Bible. First Paul reminds us of the great height from which Jesus voluntarily stepped down. "The divine nature was his from the first." Refusing to 'hang on' to His rights, Jesus for our salvation stooped lower and lower, becoming Man, becoming a slave, becoming an outcast. He accepted even death on a Roman cross. But that was not the end. He had stooped down. Now His Father raised Him up. So the passage reaches its tremendous climax with the words, "God raised Him to the heights and bestowed on him the name above all names, that at the name of Jesus every knee should bow—in heaven, on earth, and in the depths—and every tongue confess, 'Jesus Christ is Lord', to the glory of God the Father." Ascension Day is, therefore, primarily the Festival of Christ the King.

In the Bible the place at a person's right hand is very significant. We are told in 1 Kings 2:19 that King Solomon caused his mother, Bathsheba, to sit at his right hand. Here it is a position of honour. Moses says, after the Red Sea deliverance, "Thy right hand, O Lord, is become glorious in power: thy right hand, O Lord, hath dashed in pieces the enemy" (Exodus 15:6). Here the right hand is a symbol of power. It is not surprising to find, therefore, that in His exalted state Christ is seated at the Father's right hand.

His is the position of honour. As Hebrews 1:3 reminds us, "When He had brought about the purgation of sins, he took his seat at the right hand of Majesty on high, raised as far above the angels, as the title he has inherited is superior to theirs." Verse 8 of the same chapter brings home to us the honour of this position for there we find the Father saying of the Son, "Thy throne, *O God,* is for ever and ever. . . . Thou hast loved right and hated wrong; therefore, *O God,* thy God has set thee above thy fellows."

His is also the position of power. We are told in 1 Peter 3:22, "Jesus Christ . . . entered heaven after receiving the submission of angelic authorities and powers, and is now at the right hand of God". So, in anticipation of this, Christ Himself was able to say to His disciples, "Full authority in heaven and on earth has been committed to me" (Matthew 28:18).

The Ascended Christ occupies this position of honour and power. He sits as Lord of Creation, King of the Universe, Judge of the World. He occupies, in fact, the position that was His before He became Man. When He had finished the task His Father sent Him to do, He returned to His Father's right hand. Yet He returned with a difference; He has taken our human nature back with Him. There in heaven He is still God and Man. His manhood was not destroyed at the Ascension, and it was not absorbed into His deity. The mediator between God and men is still "Himself man" (1 Timothy 2:6). So Bishop Christopher Wordsworth was right when he wrote,

He has raised our human nature
On the clouds to God's right hand.

CHRIST THE ADVOCATE

Jesus Christ is now "in the presence of God for us", or "on our behalf" (Hebrews 9:24). There He is our "Advocate with the Father" (1 John 2:1), "the propitiation for our sins". In other words, having completed His earthly ministry, Christ continues His heavenly ministry. Like the advocate pleading a case in the law court, Christ pleads our case with His Father in heaven.

He does not plead in words, but by His presence. The very fact that He is there speaks loudly on our behalf. John Calvin, the Reformer, said, "He directs attention to his own righteousness so as to turn it away from our sins." As the Father looks at Christ He remembers Calvary, and as He remembers Calvary He forgives the sin of all those who come to Him in Christ's Name.

This is the only New Testament basis for salvation. This is the only ground on which we are able to stand before a holy God. But it is sufficient. When we do come in Christ's Name, cleansed by His blood and clothed in His righteousness, God looks upon us as we are seen in Christ, and He treats us as if we were righteous because in Christ *we are*. This is what is meant by justification by faith.

As usual, Paul has just the right words to sum it up. "Who will be the accuser of God's chosen ones? It is God who pronounces acquittal: then who can condemn? It is Christ —Christ who died, and, more than that, was raised from the dead—who is at God's right hand, and indeed pleads our cause" (Romans 8:33ff). Therefore, he concludes, "nothing in all creation . . . can separate us from the love of God in Christ Jesus our Lord" (Romans 8:39). Ultimately, this is what the Ascension is all about.

10

CHRIST'S RETURN

We have almost completed our study outline of the Person and Work of Christ as it appears in the Creed. What have we seen so far? The Christian Faith means faith in Jesus Christ, a Person who is both God and Man. From all eternity He existed with His Father in heaven. Then at Bethlehem, He who has always been God became Man, being born of the Virgin Mary through the power of the Holy Spirit. Having lived a perfect life, He offered Himself up as a voluntary sacrifice, dying on the cross to reconcile us to God. On the third day He rose from the dead and then ascended to the place of honour and power which He had occupied before the Incarnation. To complete the picture we must look at Christ's Second Coming.

The Apostles' Creed states, "From thence [heaven] He shall come to judge the quick and the dead." First we must consider the *fact* of His coming ("He shall come"), leaving the *purpose* of His coming ("to judge the quick and the dead") for another chapter.

A REVEALED TRUTH

How do we know that Christ will return? Before we attempt to answer that question, we need to remember that the Christian Faith is based on truth revealed by God. God has revealed Himself to the world in the Person of His Son. To know what God is like, we look at Jesus Christ. To know what God wants, we listen to Jesus Christ. In other words, all that God wants us to know about Himself is summed up for us in Jesus Christ. This is what is meant by the statement, "Christianity is Christ".

Now all that we know of Jesus Christ has been handed down to us through the apostles and is contained in the New Testament. People sometimes speak of "the Jesus of history" as if He were a figure independent of the New Testament records. Nothing could be further from the truth. The only Jesus we know is the Jesus of the New Testament. Any other 'Jesus' is a creation of our own imagination. That being so, Christianity according to Christ is the Christianity of the New Testament scriptures.

This has always been an important principle within the Church of England. "Holy Scripture containeth all things necessary to salvation: so that whatsoever is not read therein, nor may be proved thereby, is not to be required of any man, that it should be believed as an article of the Faith, or be thought requisite or necessary to salvation" (Article VI of the XXXIX Articles).

You may wonder where all this is leading. Simply to this point: we accept the doctrine of Christ's future Return in the same way that we accept the doctrines of His Incarnation, His Death, His Resurrection, and His Ascension, because like them it is an essential part of New Testament teaching.

Moreover, what the New Testament teaches the Church has accepted and confirmed. As we have seen, those responsible for the Apostles' Creed included the statement, "He shall come to judge the quick [the living] and the dead." The Nicene Creed states the same truth: "He shall come again with glory to judge both the quick and the dead." Similarly, whoever wrote the *Te Deum* stated, "We believe that Thou shalt come to be our Judge", and in the Advent Collect Cranmer reminded the Church, "In the last day he shall come again in His glorious majesty to judge both the quick and the dead."

I have included these quotations to show that belief in Christ's Second Coming is not something foreign to the

Church of England. Many Anglicans fight shy of this subject altogether, because of the way in which some heretical movements distort the New Testament teaching. But, as we have seen, a glance through the Prayer Book shows that belief in Christ's return has always been part of orthodox Anglicanism. It should be remembered, though, that the relevant scriptures are open to more than one interpretation. We should beware of those who claim to know all the answers, even down to the actual date of Christ's Return. Even Christ Himself confessed ignorance on this last point!

Although it is true that no one interpretation of the Second Coming is necessarily the correct one, there are certain basic ideas running right through the New Testament. Here we can do no more than look briefly at one or two of them.

A PERSONAL RETURN

The New Testament writers see Christ's Return as a personal one. Christ promised, "I will come again" (John 14:3). Some people believe this promise was fulfilled when the Spirit came on the day of Pentecost (Acts 2), but although there is a sense in which Christ did indeed become spiritually real to the disciples after the outpouring of the Spirit, it remains true that even after Pentecost the New Testament writers are still looking forward to Christ's Return. Some Christians expected the Second Coming to occur during their own lifetime, and gave up their employment in anticipation of this. Paul had to use strong words to urge them to return to their daily occupations (2 Thessalonians 3:10). This mistaken attitude shows how sure they were that Christ would return. The verse which best sums up this idea of a Personal Return of Christ is Acts 1:11, "This Jesus, who has been taken away from you up to heaven, will come in the same way as you have seen him go."

A VISIBLE RETURN

Christ's Return will be visible as well as personal. This is implied in Acts 1:11. Christ Himself was more explicit: "They will see the Son of Man coming on the clouds of heaven with great power and glory" (Matthew 24:30). Paul, too, had no doubts about it: "The Lord himself will descend from heaven" (1 Thessalonians 4:16).

AN UNEXPECTED RETURN

In the same context, Paul shows that the coming of Christ will be unexpected in the sense that it will be unheralded and therefore will take many people by surprise. He writes, "About dates and times, my friends, we need not write to you, for you know perfectly well that the Day of the Lord comes like a thief in the night. While they are talking of peace and security, all at once calamity is upon them, sudden as the pangs that come upon a woman with child; and there will be no escape. But you, my friends, are not in the dark, that the day should overtake you like a thief. You are all children of light, children of day. We do not belong to night or darkness, and we must not sleep like the rest, but keep awake and be sober" (1 Thessalonians 5:1–6).

This idea occurs in several of Christ's parables (e.g. Matthew 24:45ff, and 25:1ff) and on more than one occasion Christ gave the express warning, "Keep awake then; for you never know the day or the hour" (Matthew 24:42, 25:13).

THE END—OR THE BEGINNING?

In our next chapter we shall see that the Second Coming of Christ will usher in the Day of Judgement. But it should be remembered that it will also usher in the Day of Consummation. However we interpret the prophetic passages of a new heaven and a new earth, this much is clear—when the Lord returns the Kingdom of God will come in all its fullness. As Dr. J. S. Whale has written, "Christian doctrine will have nothing to do with an earthly eternity for the human race, as though the city of God were the goal of secular evolution here on this planet, where man will live happily ever afterwards. . . . The only true evaluation of this world is one which recognises the impermanence of this world. Here we have no abiding city: we seek one that is beyond history and beyond death. We are always strangers and sojourners; our citizenship is in heaven" (*Christian Doctrine*, p. 169).

QUESTIONS

1. Look up the following passages: Matthew 25, Acts 1:6–11, 1 Thessalonians 5:1–11, 2 Peter 3:1–13. What *facts* do they give concerning the Second Coming of Christ?
2. How often is the Second Coming mentioned in the service of Morning Prayer?

11

CHRIST'S JUDGEMENT

When Christ came in humility nearly two thousand years ago, He came to save. When He comes again in power at the end of the world, He will come to judge. So the Apostles' Creed states, "He shall come to judge the quick and the dead." The 'quick' are simply the living, those still alive when Christ returns, the others being those whose death has preceded His return.

A NEW TESTAMENT EMPHASIS

In stating that Christ will return to judge, the Creed is simply echoing the teaching of the New Testament. Peter told the Caesareans, Christ "is the one who has been designated by God as judge of the living and the dead" (Acts 10:42). Paul concluded his sermon to the men of Athens with the words, "God commands mankind, all men everywhere, to repent, because he has fixed the day on which he will have the world judged, and justly judged, by a man of his choosing; of this he has given assurance to all by raising him from the dead" (Acts 17:31). The same apostle wrote to the Corinthians, "We must all have our lives laid open before the tribunal of Christ, where each must receive what is due to him for his conduct in the body, good or bad" (2 Corinthians 5:10). Elsewhere Paul shows that this coming judgement is linked with the Second Coming of Christ, for he tells Timothy, "Before God, and before Christ Jesus who is to judge all men living and dead, I adjure you by his coming appearance and reign, proclaim the message'' (2 Timothy 4:1).

This teaching sprang naturally from what Christ had taught earlier. He spoke of His Second Coming as a time of separation—wheat from tares, sheep from goats, good from evil (Matthew 13:24ff, 25:31ff). In the parable of the Ten Virgins He warned His hearers of the need to be ready for His return (Matthew 25:1–13), the punch-line coming in the last verse, ''Keep awake then; for you never know the day or the hour.'' Chapters 24 and 25 of Matthew will repay careful study.

The challenge of all this is clear. We must be ready all the time, if we are to be ready at the time. When Christ returns we shall have to submit our individual accounts to His scrutiny. Then, dependent upon the verdict He will then give, we shall spend eternity either in the presence of God (the blessed state which the Bible calls heaven), or we shall be shut out of His presence for ever (a fearful state which the Bible calls hell).

SOME OBJECTIONS CONSIDERED

Not everyone is prepared to accept the idea of Christ coming to judge and the implications regarding our ultimate destiny. Here are some of the objections raised.

''Surely if God is love, He will not send anyone to hell.'' In answer, we must re-word the question, so that it runs ''Surely God will not force anyone to love Him and spend eternity with Him in heaven.'' God has made us in such a way that we may respond freely to His love, but this means we also have freedom to reject His love. David Read maintains, therefore, ''The traditional Christian doctrine of hell is actually one of the strongest affirmations of man's free-will known to human thought, for it contemplates the possibility of one of God's creatures being able to say No to Him indefinitely.'' He adds, ''God does not damn us. We damn ourselves'' (*The Christian Faith*, p. 100).

''What about the people who have never heard the Gospel?'' On this point the Bible is silent. However, we are shown enough of God's character to make us realise that He will not condemn people for failing to respond to a Gospel they have never heard. It should be remembered, however, that this objection is usually made by people who have had every opportunity of hearing and heeding the message but of their own free-will have refused to repent and believe in Christ. About them, the Bible is quite explicit. Much will be required of those to whom much is given.

"Why must we decide now? Surely there will be another chance in the next life." The Bible encourages no such hope. It stresses rather the importance of deciding aright and living aright now, for "The hour of favour has now come; now, I say, has the day of deliverance dawned" (2 Corinthians 6:2). In any case, as Dr. C. B. Moss pointed out, "The kind of person who hopes for a second chance would, if he were given one, hope for a third chance, and so on" (*The Christian Faith*, p. 453).

Perhaps the last word on this solemn subject is best given to the report, *Doctrine in the Church of England*. This official Anglican document states, "The doctrine of Judgement pervades the whole of Scripture, alike in the Old Testament and in the New." It warns against "the easy-going sentimentality of some modern Christianity" (p. 216ff). The Apostles' Creed urges us to heed the warning, for whenever we repeat it it warns us Christ "shall come to judge the living and the dead".

QUESTIONS

1. "Pie in the sky when you die." Is this a valid criticism of the Gospel?
2. "A God of love wouldn't condemn anyone." Discuss.

FURTHER READING

John 3:16–21.
John 5:24.

12

THE HOLY SPIRIT

Every Sunday thousands of Anglicans say, "I believe in the Holy Ghost." How many of them understand what they mean? What do the words 'Holy Spirit' mean to you? Do you think of the Spirit as a blind, impersonal force, something like electricity? Do you imagine a ghostly figure existing in a mysterious and shadowy world? If your ideas are Biblical, you will think of Him as a divine Person, as real and as powerful as the Father and the Son. He is the third Person of the Trinity. Soon we shall consider the relationship existing between Father, Son and Spirit. For the moment we concentrate on the Person and Work of the Holy Spirit.

Three important passages dealing with our subject are John 14:15–26, 15:26–27, and 16:7–15. Read these carefully before proceeding with this chapter.

WHO IS THE SPIRIT?

A Person

The Holy Spirit is a real Person, distinct from the Father and the Son. Though He came to take the place of the ascended Christ, He is essentially *another* Advocate (John 14:16). He comes from Christ and His Father (John 14:26, 15:26), so the Nicene Creed is correct when it states He proceeds from the Father and the Son. He came to glorify Christ (John 16:14).

Some people make the mistake of referring to the Spirit as 'it', rather than 'He'. In contrast, notice how often the New

English Bible uses personal pronouns of the Spirit in John 14–16. I counted 'he' seventeen times, 'him' four times, 'whom' twice, and 'who' once: twenty-four personal pronouns in twenty-three verses concerning the Spirit.

The fact that the Spirit is a Person is demonstrated by the very nature of His work. It is the work of a Person, not the outworkings of a blind, mechanical and impersonal force. Thus He is described as the Advocate who takes the place of the physical Christ (John 14:15), who teaches and reminds the disciples (14:26), who bears witness to Christ (15:26), and who convicts the world, guides the disciples, and glorifies Christ (16:8ff).

That the Spirit is a Person is an aspect of Christian doctrine which needs to be stressed. A number of young people were asked to say the first thing they thought of when 'Holy Spirit' was mentioned. One replied, "A sort of oblong blur." I remember that as a lad singing in a church choir I used to think that the Paraclete was some kind of bird! (It is, of course, the Greek word translated 'Advocate' in John 14:16, 14:26, 15:26, and 16:7.)

Of course it can be argued that 'Person' is not a good word to use of the Spirit, or indeed of God at all. Certainly the word has its limitations—so have all words when we are trying to describe God. But whilst we acknowledge this it is difficult to see what other word could be used to describe the Spirit, who is distinct from the Father and Son and who works in a personal way. As long as we do not ascribe to Him the limitations of imperfect human personality, 'Person' is as good a word as any.

A Divine Person

The disciples were told that the Spirit would make up to them what they were losing by Christ's departure (John 14:14ff). He was to become to them Christ's 'Other Self'. (In this respect it is right to think of another coming of Christ when the Spirit came, though, as we have seen in a previous chapter, there is still a very real sense in which the Second Coming of Christ is an event to which we look forward.)

John 14:23 goes even further, showing that when the Spirit comes to dwell in a person, it may be said that the Father and the Son dwell in that person. The Spirit's presence means God's presence, the Spirit's activity means God's activity.

We may sum up what we have seen so far in three statements.

1. The Holy Spirit is a Person.
2. The Holy Spirit is a Divine Person.
3. The Holy Spirit makes real the presence of God in the heart of the Christian.

WHAT IS THE WORK OF THE SPIRIT?

The Holy Spirit is God in action—but in action in what way, and for what purpose? His title 'Advocate' gives us an insight into His ministry. Readers familiar with Television's Perry Mason will not need to be told that the advocate's task is to plead a cause. The Greek word for Advocate (*paracletos*, from which we get the title Paraclete) is found only five times in the New Testament, of Christ in 1 John 2:1 and of the Spirit in John 14:16, 14:26, 15:26, and 16:7.

In the Epistle we are told, "We have an Advocate with the Father, Jesus Christ the righteous: and he is the propitiation for our sins." In the New English Bible it is translated, "We have one to plead our cause with the Father, Jesus Christ, and he is just. He is himself the remedy for the defilement of our sins." This reminds us that the Christ who died for our sins and rose triumphantly on the third day, is now "in the presence of God for us" (Hebrews 9:24) and there pleads our cause with the Father (See chapter 9).

The Spirit's advocacy, however, is in the opposite direction. Whereas Christ pleads our cause with the Father, the Spirit pleads Christ's cause with us. The advocacy of the Lord Jesus Christ is directed towards God on our behalf: the advocacy of the Holy Spirit is directed towards us on God's behalf. What God now has to say to us He says through the Spirit.

The Spirit and Holiness

To be holy means to be *set apart from* all that is of Satan and evil and to be *consecrated to* all that is of God and good. In one sense, every Christian *is* holy. He has been set apart from sin and has become consecrated to God. That is why the New Testament calls Christians 'saints'. But the New Testament goes on to urge us to become saints, that is to grow in holiness day by day.

The Holy Spirit is the One who enables us to achieve this. He does not do this by giving us a kind of 'instant holiness'. He does it by working in us and through us, and usually as we make use of the means of grace God has given us, prayer, Bible reading, worship and Christian fellowship. As the Spirit works, His work becomes evident in our lives. So Paul can say, "The harvest of the Spirit is love, joy, peace, patience, kindness, goodness, fidelity, gentleness, and self-control" (Galatians 5:22). It will be seen, therefore, that holiness in the New Testament sense of that word is far removed from superficial piety, smugness, and a sense of one's own superiority. Holiness is simply Christianity applied to the whole of one's life. Holiness is, in fact, the kind of life that Jesus lived.

The Spirit and Scripture

Christ is God's Incarnate Word; the Bible is God's written Word. All that God says to us in Christ is enshrined for us in the Bible. Peter was quick to see that the Old Testament scriptures had been written by men moved by the Spirit (2 Peter 1:21). Paul stated that "All Scripture is inspired by God" (2 Timothy 3:16). The Early Church recognised that a similar divine authority lay behind the writings of the New Testament. Similarly, the Church of England acknowledges that Christian doctrine is essentially that which the Bible teaches (see chapter 3). This is why corporate Bible study should have an important place in a church's programme and why private Bible reading should be a priority in the life of every Christian.

Now the Spirit who inspired the ancient writers of the

Bible is the One who enlightens us as we read the Bible. The Holy Spirit is the One who makes the book live to us. Without His work, Bible reading is simply an intellectual exercise. With His aid, Bible reading becomes a spiritual exercise, a means of grace. He makes the book live, and then He gives us the strength to apply its teaching in our daily lives.

The Spirit and Evangelism

Christ promised His disciples, "You will receive power when the Holy Spirit comes upon you; and you will bear witness for me" (Acts 1:8). It was not until this promise had been fulfilled that Peter and the others became effective witnesses for Christ. Later, Paul wrote, "No one can say 'Jesus is Lord' except under the influence of the Holy Spirit" (1 Corinthians 12:3). The Holy Spirit is still the dynamic of Christian evangelism, and although He works in and through Christians (and sometimes in spite of them!), no one is converted to the Christian faith without His work. An effective church is not just a well-organised church but a Spirit-filled church and the same is true of an effective Christian.

The Spirit and the Church

The Church is the sphere in which the Holy Spirit normally works, and often He does so through the Church's ordinances, as we shall consider when we discuss the sacraments. But this is not to claim that the Spirit does not work outside the Church. Who are we to limit God Almighty? He is, however, the Spirit of the Church and it is normally through the Church that His blessings come to us.

QUESTION

Look through the Whitsuntide section of a hymn book. Does it give a biblical view of the Person and work of the Holy Spirit?

FURTHER READING

John 14:15–26.
John 15:26–27.
John 16:7–15.

13

THE TRINITY

"I believe in God the Father . . . and in Jesus Christ . . . (and) in the Holy Ghost." These are the three most important statements of the Apostles' Creed. Already we have seen that the Christian Faith means faith in these three Persons, and we have looked at each individually. Now we must consider the relationship that exists between them in the unity of the Godhead. That relationship may be expressed as follows. There is only one God: yet within the unity of the Godhead there are three Persons—Father, Son, and Holy Spirit. Although each person is truly God, there is only one God—not three.

Before we consider how Christians arrived at this view of God, we need to remember two facts. First, we know what God is like only because He has revealed Himself to us. To say that there are three divine Persons but only one God is our attempt to express God's great self-disclosure in inadequate human language.

Secondly, we need to remember that God is infinite and we are finite. We can hardly expect our puny minds to be able to grasp (and even contain) all there is to know about God. He is, after all, Perfect Mind. A legend about St. Augustine of Hippo illustrates the point. This great theologian was walking along a beach when he saw a boy emptying sea-water into a hole in the sand. "What are you doing?" asked Augustine. "I'm emptying the sea into this hole," answered the boy. "How can you empty the sea into that little hole?" challenged Augustine. Whereupon the boy, who, so the legend explains, was really an angel in disguise, replied, "And how can you understand the doctrine of the Trinity with your finite human mind?" We take the point and move on with caution!

FACT OF GOD'S UNITY

Christians are monotheists. Like Jews we accept the statement, "The Lord our God is one Lord" (Deuteronomy 6:4). Paul, the Jew who had become a Christian, could still write, "There is one God" (1 Timothy 2:5). The first Christians were as appalled as were the Jews by the polytheism and idolatry of their pagan Greek neighbours. But these first Christians were faced with two facts which led them to think of the one God existing eternally in three Persons. These two facts were the fact of Christ and the fact of the Holy Spirit.

THE FACT OF CHRIST

The first disciples knew Christ as a man, living and working among men. As time passed, however, they were compelled to see that, although truly man, He was not merely man. His life, His claims, His miracles, and finally the vindication of His resurrection led them to think of Him as God. Thomas seems to have been speaking for all of them when he cried, "My Lord and my God!" (John 20:28), an estimate of His Person which Jesus Himself accepted. Certainly the writer of the Fourth Gospel had no doubt of Christ's diety, for he wrote, "When all things began, the Word already was. The Word dwelt with God, and what God was, the Word was" (John 1:1). On the other hand, Jesus was obviously distinct from the Father (He was not the same Person), for He said He had been sent by His Father to do His Father's will and that when it was accomplished He would return to His Father.

THE FACT OF THE HOLY SPIRIT

Their experience of the Holy Spirit after the first Whit Sunday convinced the first Christians that they had to reckon with Him as a divine Person who dwelt within them. But again, they did not confuse the Spirit with the Father or the Son. He was a distinct Person, for had Jesus not told them that the Spirit would come to take His place and would be sent by the Father?

THREE PERSONS—ONE GOD

Here, then, was the problem facing the first Christians. They believed there was only one God. Jesus had taught them they had a Father in heaven. They had come to recognise Christ Himself as a divine Person, yet they knew that He and the Father were distinct Persons. Later they recognised that the Holy Spirit was a third divine Person. How were they to reconcile their idea of one God with these new ideas of three divine Persons? They made no attempt to reconcile them, but simply stated the three ideas, and (in New Testament times at least) without comment. So Paul writes, "The grace of the Lord Jesus Christ and the love of God and the fellowship of the Holy Spirit be with you all" (2 Corinthians 13:14).

Later Christians found it necessary to state their faith in the Triune God in more precise theological language because of certain heretical teachers who were denying such a faith. The classical expression of the doctrine, the Prayer Book's Athanasian Creed, probably did not come into use until about the ninth century, but the doctrine of the Trinity was there in embryo from the beginning.

I am not going to pretend that the doctrine of the Trinity is uncomplicated. How God can be both one and three is something beyond our comprehension. But is not this what we should expect? So often we try to remake God in our own image. We try to fashion Him in a way that is acceptable to our finite minds. In doing this we tend to fall into the danger of idolatry, for the God we are then professing to worship is not the God of the Bible, the God and Father of our Lord Jesus Christ, but a 'god' we ourselves have made.

We cannot contain Him. We cannot place Him in one of our own little categories. He is the God who created the heavens and the earth. He made us. How can the clay explain the potter? He is the eternal and infinite God who defies definition. He has chosen to reveal Himself to us. We have to make the best we can of that revelation in the inadequate human vocabulary at our disposal. So we speak of three Persons, Father, Son and Spirit, but only one God.

QUESTIONS

1. What do you understand by 'the Trinity'?
2. Should we be surprised by the difficulties of this doctrine?

14

THE CHURCH

The Apostles' Creed invites us to affirm our faith in "the Holy Catholic Church". Here we have three of the most misunderstood words in the Christian vocabulary. To many people 'holy' is almost the equivalent of 'unreal'; 'catholic' indicates membership of that body whose earthly head is the Pope, and 'church' calls to mind the building round the corner where a few people go to perform certain religious rites. Before you read on, test yourself. What do you think each word means? How close are your ideas to those of the New Testament?

THE NATURE OF THE CHURCH

Consider the following three statements.

"I'm going to church."

"I'm Church, not Chapel."

"The Church should do something about it."

In each example 'church' means something different. In the first case 'church' is the building to which one goes to take part in an act of worship. In the second example the use of the word 'church' as against 'chapel' distinguishes one denomination (the Church of England) from others (Nonconformists or 'Free Churches'), a distinction still very real in certain parts of rural England. 'Church' is used in a much wider sense in the third case, for it is conceived of as a national (or perhaps universal) institution. Because of these diversities (and many other examples could have been adduced), it is important to know what we mean by the Church when we say, in the Creed, that we believe in it.

The Greek New Testament word for 'church' is *ecclesia*, from which is derived our word 'ecclesiastical'. *Ecclesia* always refers to people, never to buildings. In the New Testament period there were no church buildings. Christians met for worship and fellowship in each other's houses. The Church in Corinth (or Rome, or Ephesus, or Galatia, or anywhere else) was not a building, but a local group of believing people, the congregation of Christians. The Church did not consist of ordinary bricks and mortar but of people who were the 'living stones' of a spiritual Temple of which Christ was 'the foundation-stone' (Ephesians 2:20), 'the corner-stone' (1 Peter 2:6). Other New Testament metaphors emphasise the same truth. The Church is God's Flock, God's Household, God's Family, Christ's Bride, and Christ's Body. The word 'church' is another way of saying 'the People of God'.

The Apostles' Creed describes the Church as 'Holy' and 'Catholic'. The Nicene Creed adds the information that it is 'One' and 'Apostolic'. As we consider these four facts about the Church we shall begin to understand something of its nature.

The Church is One

We speak of the Church of England, or the Church of Scotland or the Church of Rome. People of different persuasions are described as Baptists, Methodists or Congregationalists. For years we have been conditioned into thinking that this travesty of New Testament Christianity is a legitimate demonstration of our differences of temperament. At last Christians of all denominations are beginning to recognise it as sin. There is only one Church, the Church of God, the Body of Christ. All who have faith in Christ as Saviour and acknowledge Him as Lord belong to that one Church. At present this essential unity is obscured by our unhappy divisions, but the situation is improving. Anglicans and Methodists are working towards union. Members of other Christian bodies are considering how best to heal their divisions. These are all moves in the right direction.

The New Testament Scriptures provide no justification for several competing churches. The one Church, Christ's Body, has its local manifestations, one for each locality. We may distinguish them from the *one Church* by calling them *churches*. In Acts and the Epistles we find local churches in Italy, Greece and Asia. But *the Church* proper cannot be limited to one place. It consists of "all men everywhere who invoke the name of our Lord Jesus Christ" (1 Corinthians 1:2). The New English Bible helpfully distinguishes these local churches from the one Church by calling them 'congregations'.

The Church is Holy

This does not mean that all its members are perfect. Far from it! We need to look no further than ourselves to see that such a view is manifestly absurd. The Church, consisting as it does of people like you and me, is the fellowship of forgiven sinners, the community of the redeemed. In what sense, then, may it be called holy?

The words 'holy' and 'saint' come from the same Greek root. Its basic meaning is 'set apart'. The New Testament speaks of all Christians as 'saints', for they have been 'set apart' from sin for God. They may be far from 'saintly' in behaviour, but nonetheless they have been set apart for God and therefore they are saints. In a similar way, the Church (that is the sum total of all these individual 'saints') is holy in the sense that it is 'set apart', dedicated to the service of God in the world.

The Church is Catholic

Like 'holy' and 'church', 'catholic' is a word open to misunderstanding. Members of the Roman Church call themselves 'Catholics' and some high churchmen are described as 'Anglo-Catholics'. But neither have a monopoly, for 'catholic' means 'universal'. The Church is catholic because it is universal. It has a message which all need and it embraces all who heed. "It transcends the barriers of race, language, and colour" (*Doctrine in the Church of England*, p. 102). To call the Church catholic, therefore, is to agree with Paul's words: "Through faith you are all sons of God in union with Christ Jesus. Baptised into union with him, you have all put on Christ as a garment. There is no such thing as Jew and Greek, slave and freeman, male and female; for you are all one person in Christ Jesus" (Galatians 3:26–28).

The practical implications of this are obvious. Class barriers, colour barriers or any other barriers have no place within the Christian Church. Where they are allowed to exist, the Church is forfeiting its right to be called catholic. We need not look as far away as South Africa to find examples of this.

The Church is Apostolic

'Apostle' comes from the Greek verb *apostello* which means 'to send'. An 'apostle' is 'one who has been sent' and more particularly 'one who has been sent with a particular message and for a special purpose'. The New Testament Apostles were the twelve men Jesus selected from a much wider circle of disciples to be His companions and to go out to preach and heal in His name (Mark 3:14–15). Their office was a foundational office. So Paul tells the Ephesian Christians, "You are built upon the foundation laid by the apostles and prophets" (Ephesians 2:20). Their work was unique and their office could not be transmitted. The Apostolic Church as such began and ended with the Twelve, and in this strict sense there are no Apostles in the Church today (except those in glory with Christ).

In a much more important sense, however, we cannot limit the words 'apostolic' or 'church' to any one period of history. The Church as such is the People of God, past, present, and future. Today's Church is the same as the Church that Christ originally founded with the Twelve Apostles as its nucleus. So in this historical sense the Church is apostolic.

The Church is apostolic also in the sense that the message it proclaims today is the message proclaimed by the Apostles in the first century A.D. We have to adapt our methods and organisation to suit the twentieth century, but the message itself cannot be changed. Basic human needs never alter and it is these basic needs that the Gospel meets. So in this way also the Church is apostolic, for it proclaims the Gospel of the Christ who is "the same yesterday, and today, and forever" (Hebrews 13:8). It follows from this that every Christian is an apostle. By life and lip he must witness for the Christ who has called him.

THE TASK OF THE CHURCH

We have considered the nature of the Church—that is, what the Church *is*. Now we must move on to the task of the Church—that is, what the Church *does*. Two verses from Peter provide a good starting point. The Church is "a holy priesthood, to offer spiritual sacrifices acceptable to God through Jesus Christ" (1 Peter 2:5). It is "a chosen race, a royal priesthood, a dedicated nation, and a people claimed by God for his own, to proclaim the triumphs of him who has called you out of darkness into his marvellous light" (1 Peter 2:9). From these verses we may conclude that the Church's task is to worship and to witness.

The report *Doctrine in the Church of England* agrees. "The Church exists to worship God, and bears His commission in this world to bear witness to Him, to proclaim His Gospel, to bring all mankind within the membership, range and fellowship of the Redeemed Society, and to gain for the principles involved in the Gospel, application to the conditions of human life from time to time" (p. 112). Here it is stated quite specifically that the witness of the Church will involve not merely the proclamation of the Gospel message but the application of the Gospel principles to Society at large. The Church must not only talk but act.

Karl Barth spells out the implications in his *Evangelical Theology*. He says that the Church testifies to the Word in the world in five ways:

1. By the very fact of its existence in the world.

2. By its attitude to world problems.
3. By its service to all the handicapped, weak and needy.
4. By its prayer life.
5. By its spoken words—when it "attempts to make its faith audible" (pp. 184ff).

It does not require much effort to see how all this applies to the individual member of the Church. His task, like that of the Church as a whole, is to worship and to witness. It follows, therefore, that as a member of the Church

1. He must meet regularly with his fellow-Christians to worship God, especially at the service of Holy Communion instituted by Christ Himself.
2. He must persevere in his own personal prayer life.
3. He must be especially concerned (as was his Master) for the sick, the suffering, and the under-privileged, whether they are found in his own country or overseas.
4. He must witness for Christ by the way he lives, allowing what he believes to affect the way he behaves.
5. He must seek opportunity to back up the witness of his life with the witness of his lips.

It goes without saying that he will be the better encouraged to do all these things if he is a member of a live church and a loving fellowship.

QUESTIONS

1. Which is more important, worship or witness?
2. How would you answer the person who says, "I don't go to church, but I'm just as good as those who do."?

FURTHER READING

What is the Church Here For?, M. Saward (Falcon Booklet).

15

THE GOSPEL SACRAMENTS

Visual aids have always played an important part in education. What we see as well as hear we are twice as likely to remember as what we only hear. Modern advertising techniques and especially the advent of television have merely underlined this fact. Today local education authorities employ specialists in audio-visual techniques to advise their teachers how best to appeal to their pupils through 'eye-gate' as well as 'ear-gate'. In every well equipped school there is a readily-available supply of audio-visual equipment.

Jesus, the supreme Teacher of all times, was an expert story-teller, a master of the spoken word. He did not neglect visual aids—some of His best parables were probably inspired by what He and His hearers saw around them at the spot where He was teaching. A poverty-striken widow and fields of ripe corn were but two of the many visual aids He employed in His ministry. His most important visual aids, however, were the two Sacraments He commanded His followers to use.

Not that Baptism and Holy Communion are merely visual aids. They are intended to do more than instruct. These two Sacraments of the Gospel portray visually the Redemption which Christ purchased on the Cross and are aids to enable believers to enter more fully into what He then achieved on their behalf.

Article XXV says that Sacraments are not only 'badges or tokens of Christian men's professional'' but rather "sure witnesses and effectual signs of grace, and God's good will towards us". By them He works invisibly in us and quickens, strengthens, and confirms our faith in Him. The Article goes on to stress the importance of faith on the part of the recipient of the Sacraments. "In such only as worthily receive the same they have a wholesome effect or operation."

The definition in the Revised Catechism is a little simpler. "By the sacrament I mean the use of material things as signs and pledges of God's grace, and as a means by which we receive his gifts." It goes on to give the well-known description of the two parts of a sacrament, "The outward and visible sign, and the inward and spiritual grace." The outward and visible sign in Baptism is water and the inward and spiritual gift is "union with Christ in his death and resurrection, the forgiveness of sins, and a new birth into God's family, the Church". The outward and visible sign in Holy Communion is the bread and wine and the inward and spiritual gift is "the Body and Blood of Christ, truly and indeed given by him and received by the faithful".

16

THE SACRAMENT OF BAPTISM

The Prayer Book contains three Baptismal services. Two of them are public services, one for adults and the other for infants, and the other is the private Baptism for Infants, intended for use only in an emergency. The Church of England has now authorised for experimental use alternative Baptism services in booklet form, and these are obtainable from S.P.C.K. Leaving aside emergency baptism, the others contain the following elements: the reading of Scriptures, the making of promises, the actual baptism itself, declarations of regeneration and Church membership, and a welcome into the Christian community, all in the context of prayer offered by believing people.

A GOSPEL SACRAMENT

Like Holy Communion, Baptism is a Sacrament of the Gospel. It was appointed by Christ for His Church. As a Gospel Sacrament, it can be understood only in the light of the Christian Gospel as a whole. That Gospel states that man is a sinner who cannot save himself, that God sent His Son to live, die, and rise again in order that sinners might be saved, and that for those who come to God in Christ there is forgiveness, new life, and restored fellowship with God. Part of this Gospel proclamation is read at every Baptism service.

Naturally it is assumed that it is the blessings of the Gospel that the people want. If not then it is difficult to see how the administration of Baptism to them or their children can be justified. The New Testament makes it quite clear that the blessings of the Gospel come to us when we repent and put our trust in Christ, and it warns us that the reality of faith is judged not by how it talks but by how it behaves (James 2). Because of this Baptism requires the promise of such a response, from the adult candidate on his own behalf and from the parents and sponsors on the infant's part, and it is only when this promise has been made that the Sacrament is administered.

The Prayer Book services are quite clear as to the kind of response required. There must be a renouncing of the devil and all his works, a profession of Christian faith as summarised in the Apostles' Creed, and a promise of obedience to God's will and commandments. The Alternative Services (Series 2) are even more specific. Candidates for Baptism (or in the case of infants their parents and sponsors) have to promise that they do in fact turn to Christ, repent of their sins, renounce evil, and believe and trust in God the Father who made the world, Jesus Christ His Son who redeemed mankind, and God's Holy Spirit who sanctifies the people of God. The fact that such responses now have to be made publicly, in the presence of a representative congregation of the local church, and after due preparation, means that the practice of Baptism is less open to abuse than previously.

AN EFFECTUAL SIGN

The method of Baptism is identical for infants and adults. The candidates may be dipped in water or have it poured over them. The action takes place in the Name of the Father, the Son, and the Holy Spirit.

The water used is ordinary water. It becomes 'holy' only in the technical sense that after prayer it is water that has been set apart from ordinary use for a specific spiritual purpose. There is nothing magical about it. It has changed its purpose not its nature. The grace that is available in Baptism comes from God, not from the water.

In Baptism we are using water as a sign and pledge of God's grace, and as a means by which we receive His gifts (see the Revised Catechism). If you like, the water is a visual aid, an object lesson. But although God is using a material thing, we must not think that His grace comes to us in any mechanical way. Baptism is effective in that it directs our attention to the Christ who died and rose for us. It becomes personally effective for us when we so identify ourselves with Christ that we die to sin and rise to new life in Him. So the blessings of the Christian Gospel come to us through faith in Christ, not through confidence in 'things'. We must never divorce Baptism from Christ as if the Sacrament provided us with an optional method of obtaining God's grace. Baptism is an acted sermon, or (in Augustine's expression) a 'visible word'. Like every other word of God it has to be heeded. Its message is that Christ died for us and that Christ rose for us. As we receive that message we look beyond the Sacrament to Christ, and as we receive Him in faith we obtain God's grace.

In the warm climate of the Middle East, Baptism usually took place in a river or lake and the candidates were totally immersed. Before each person was baptised he would confess "Jesus Christ is Lord". As he was lowered into the water, he would remember that Christ died for him to wash away his sin. As he was lifted out of the water, he would remember that Christ rose for him and offered him new life and the power to live it. This is what Paul had in mind in Romans 6:3–4: "Have you forgotten that when you were baptised into union with Christ Jesus we were baptised into his death? By baptism we were buried with him and lay dead, in order that, as Christ was raised from the dead in the splendour of the Father, so also we might set our feet upon the new path of life." Baptism has not lost its significance. It means for us what it meant to the early Christians, death to sin and new life in Christ. But obviously this 'death' and 'resurrection' take place only through faith. This is why the Church of England requires evidence of faith from those who come for this Sacrament.

CHRISTIAN INITIATION

In the Prayer Book service, immediately after Baptism the candidate is received into "the congregation of Christ's flock" and is signed with the sign of the cross on his forehead "in token that hereafter he shall not be ashamed to confess the faith of Christ crucified, and manfully to fight under his banner against sin, the world, and the devil; and to continue Christ's faithful soldier and servant unto his life's end". In the Alternative Service (Series 2), the whole congregation joins in this reception of the new members. Then they may add, "God has received you by Baptism into his Church. We therefore welcome you into the Lord's family, as fellow-members of the Body of Christ, as children of the same heavenly Father, as inheritors with us of the kingdom of God."

All this underlines the fact that Baptism is the Sacrament of initiation, the formal sign of admission to the Christian Church. The candidate has signed on, he has been enrolled. He has had his feet placed firmly on the road of Christian service within the fellowship of God's People, the Body of Christ. It is not going to be an easy road to travel. He will need the very best qualities of the loyal soldier and the faithful servant if he is to persevere. But through the power of the Holy Spirit within the fellowship of the Christian Church he will find the grace of continuance.

INFANT BAPTISM

We have stressed the importance of faith. God has acted on our behalf in Christ. We must appropriate the blessings that are thus available to us in Christ by putting our trust in Him. But, some will urge, infants are incapable of such faith. How then can we justify Infant Baptism?

It cannot be stated too strongly that there is no scriptural justification for *indiscriminate* infant Baptism. Some parents regard Baptism as a ticket to heaven, and to allow them to continue uncorrected in this superstition is to endanger the eternal spiritual well-being of both them and their children. Other parents regard Baptism as a sign of social respectability, or as an official naming ceremony, or as a prelude to a christening party. For years the Church of England has been discussing these abuses. Now slowly it is beginning to act. In the Diocese of Chelmsford, for example, the Bishop, after full discussion with clergy and laity in Synod, has put forward a policy for Infant Baptism which includes careful preparation for those concerned, administration during a normal church service, and the provision of a service of thanksgiving, naming, and blessing of children when parents cannot sincerely make the promises required in the Baptism service.

The justification for bringing infants to be baptised is that the parents concerned are practising Christians and intend to bring up their children in a Christian home as Christians. Having made that statement, we must now consider if there is anything in the Bible to justify it.

There is no proof text either way—there is no text forbidding the Baptism of infants, and there is no text which enjoins their Baptism. If there were either, there would be no need for discussion; the question would be settled one way or the other. Our doctrine of infant Baptism, therefore, must come from what the Bible implies, rather than what it states categorically. We must ask, what is the teaching of the Bible regarding children and their relationship to God?

We must take into account the whole Bible. Because God is absolutely consistent and utterly reliable, we shall expect to find that the God of the Old Testament is the same as the God of the New Testament and that His attitude towards children in the New Testament will be consistent with His attitude towards children in the Old Testament.

The Old Testament Background

Abraham is a good example to begin with. Romans 4:3 shows us that Abraham did not earn his salvation but, like the Christian, was justified by faith. "Abraham put his faith in

God, and that faith was counted to him as righteousness." After his 'conversion' he received as a sign and seal of his faith the ordinance of circumcision, in effect a sacrament, an outward and visible sign of an inward and spiritual grace. So Paul says, "He later received the symbolic rite of circumcision as the hall-mark of the righteousness which faith had given him when he was still uncircumcised" (Romans 4:11). In other words, Abraham was first 'converted' (came to a position of faith) and was then circumcised (received the sacrament of his conversion). In this respect he did not differ from the modern Baptist Christian who is not baptised until, as an adult, he professes his personal faith in Christ.

But what about Abraham's children? They were circumcised before they had reached the age when they were capable of consciously deciding on their own behalf to serve God. Isaac was eight days old when he was circumcised. He was far too young to have any conscious faith in God. Nevertheless, by God's command he was circumcised, for we read in Genesis 21:4, "Abraham circumcised his son Isaac when he was eight days old, as God had commanded him." Why? The answer lies in the very nature of the covenant relationship that existed between God and Abraham.

We learn about this Covenant relationship in Genesis 17. God, on His own initiative, chose Abraham. Moreover, God made this covenant not only with Abraham but also with all Abraham's descendants. "I will establish my covenant between me and thee and thy seed after thee throughout their generations for an everlasting covenant, to be a God unto thee, and to thy seed after thee. . . . And as for thee, thou shalt keep my covenant, thou, and thy seed after thee throughout their generations. This is my covenant, which ye shall keep, between me and you and thy seed after thee . . . every male among you shall be circumcised. . . . He that is eight days old shall be circumcised" (Genesis 17:7ff).

So Abraham first believed, and then received the sign of circumcision, whereas Isaac, his son, first received the sign and later believed. Father Abraham saw to it that his son

Isaac learnt what the sign meant and taught him to claim by faith what his circumcision symbolised.

This practice of infant circumcision continued right through the Old Testament. Jesus was circumcised when he was eight days old; so was John the Baptist, and so were all the male Jews. They received this covenant sign (if you like, this 'sacrament') not because of any public declaration of personal faith in God, but because they were all children of Jewish parents and therefore were born within the covenant family of God.

It did not mean that they became good Israelites, 'converted' Jews. They did not all grow up to have a right relationship with God. On the contrary Jewish history shows that at any given time only a minority remained faithful to God. But there is never any suggestion that they should not have been circumcised in the first place. Their sin was not that they were circumcised, but that being circumcised they refused to grasp all that God was holding out to them in this covenant sign. So we find verses such as Deuteronomy 10:16 and Jeremiah 4:4 calling upon those who had been physically circumcised to become spiritually circumcised. They were to circumcise their *hearts*. In effect the challenge was, "You have the sign. Now get the reality. Enter into all that the sign signifies."

New Testament Evidence

That is the Old Testament background. What happens as we turn to the New Testament? As we should expect, the early Christians (who were all Jews) carried over these ideas into Christianity. They had been brought up to believe that children had a share in the covenant. They clung to this belief. Moreover, Christ did nothing to correct them. Nowhere does He indicate that God's attitude to children is to be any different from His attitude in Old Testament days. In fact, the New Testament underlines what we have seen in the Old Testament.

When Christ's disciples would have kept parents from bringing their children to Christ, our Lord rebuked them.

"Let the children come to me; do not try to stop them; for the kingdom of God belongs to such as these. I tell you, whoever does not accept the kingdom of God like a child will never enter it" (Mark 10:14–15). Before blessing them Our Lord said that, far from being unable to receive His blessing and share in His kingdom, their very helplessness was an example of the quality required in all who would be Christians. These children, for all their immaturity and ignorance, were nearer the truth than those who had "reached years of discretion". If this is so, how can children be denied the sign of the covenant when it is perfectly possible for them to be enjoying the blessings of the covenant?

Next look at Acts 2:37ff. After Peter's great sermon on the day of Pentecost, many of his hearers were convicted of sin and cried out, "What are we to do?" Peter's reply was very significant. "Repent and be baptised, every one of you, in the name of Jesus the Messiah for the forgiveness of your sins; and you will receive the gift of the Holy Spirit. For the promise is to you *and to your children.*" To his Jewish hearers such words would mean only one thing. As under the old covenant their children were circumcised, so under the new covenant their children were to be baptised with them.

That the children of Christian parents are in a special covenant relationship with God is further illustrated by Paul's words in 1 Corinthians 7:14. "The heathen husband now belongs to God through his Christian wife, and the heathen wife through her Christian husband. Otherwise your children would not belong to God, whereas in fact they do." Whatever else this difficult verse means, it indicates at least that children with one Christian parent are not in the same category as those who have no Christian parentage. They have been born within the covenant.

The Biblical evidence points to the fact that the Old Testament covenant signs of circumcision and the Passover have now been superseded by the New Testament covenant signs of Baptism and Holy Communion. Just as circumcision was administered to children because their parents were Jews, so Baptism should be administered to children whose parents are Christians. This does not mean that the children will automatically grow up to *be* Christians. Just as Jewish children had to be taught to enter into all that circumcision signified, so Christian children have to be taught to enter into all that Baptism signifies.

The practical implications of all this for the administration of Baptism are obvious. They are summed up admirably in the Preface to the Infant Baptism Service of Series 2. "It is the practice of the Church of England to admit to Baptism those who are not old enough to profess the Christian faith. But this is done on the understanding that they will receive a Christian upbringing. This means they will be taught the Christian religion and encouraged to practise it, until such time as they present themselves to the Bishop for Confirmation, and publicly profess the faith in which they have been baptised."

FURTHER READING

Baptism Into Christ, A. M. Stibbs (Falcon Booklet).

17

THE SACRAMENT OF HOLY COMMUNION

Holy Communion and Baptism are the two Sacraments of the Gospel. They were given by Christ to His Church. Just as the elaborate sacrificial system of the Old Testament pointed forward to the Cross of Christ, these two Gospel Sacraments point back to that event. What Jesus did at Calvary gives meaning to Holy Communion and Baptism. Neither can be understood apart from the Cross. There is, however, an important difference between them. Whereas Baptism takes place only once, Holy Communion must be used regularly as a constant reminder of the redemption Christ purchased for us. The most important of the new privileges available to the confirmed person is the tremendous privilege of joining fellow Christians to receive the Sacrament.

THE IMPORTANCE OF THE SACRAMENT

We observe Holy Communion because our Lord instituted it and then commanded His followers to observe it regularly until His Second Coming. So Paul, writing to the Corinthian Christians about Holy Communion, said, "Every time you eat this bread and drink the cup, you proclaim the death of the Lord, until he comes" (I Corinthians 11:26). The importance of Holy Communion stems from this fact. It is the one service of Christian worship that has the direct authority of Christ behind it. This is not to belittle Morning or Evening Prayer. Though not enjoined by Christ, these two Prayer Book services have much to commend them and are scriptural in form and content. They should occupy an important place in the life of the Anglican Christian. But Holy Communion is more important. It must be regarded as the priority, for in it we obey our Lord's direct commandment, "Do this as a memorial of me" (1 Corinthians 11:24).

Because of what was regarded as an unbalanced emphasis on this Sacrament in the past, some Christians were rather suspicious of it and tended to neglect it. Happily, these suspicions are now being thrown off and more churches are making Holy Communion the chief of their Sunday services. The old early morning Communion for the few and the 'mangled Mattins' with abbreviated Holy Communion tacked on to the end are gradually disappearing. This is all to the good and certainly helps the newly confirmed. They come to a real act of worship, complete with hymns, psalms, lessons and sermon, as well as the Sacrament itself. They find the local Christians 'on parade', as Bishop Joost de Blank used to speak of it, taking part in the Lord's service on the Lord's Day. In a much more realistic manner, they are made to feel part of Christ's Body. In this way they receive great encouragement, something denied to many of their predecessors who (like the writer) found themselves taking Holy Communion as an 'optional extra' for a handful of keener Christians. The new Series 2 Communion service has been a tremendous help in this direction. The value of this return to the New Testament pattern cannot be exaggerated, for in the Sacrament we are taken to the very heart of the Christian Gospel.

THE MEANING OF THE SACRAMENT

The various names given to the Sacrament help to focus attention on what it should mean to those taking part.

In 1 Corinthians 11:20 it is called *the Lord's Supper*, a title retained in the Prayer Book but dropped in the Series 2 service. Better than any other title, this one recalls the actual institution at the Last Supper (Matthew 26:26–29). It also reminds us that this Sacrament is a fellowship meal, a love feast, at which all Christians, no matter what cultural, racial, social or educational backgrounds they represent, recognise their essential unity in Christ. Better than any other event in the church's programme, the Lord's Supper should demonstrate the truth of Paul's words to the Galatians, "Through faith you are all sons of God in union with Christ Jesus. Baptised into union with him, you have all put on Christ as a garment. There is no such thing as Jew and Greek, slave and freeman, male and female; for you are all one person in Christ Jesus" (Galatians 3:28).

The symbolism of the *one* loaf and the *one* cup emphasises this one-ness of all Christians at the Lord's Table. So do some of the sections included in the Series 2 service. "We are the Body of Christ", the priest may say. "By one Spirit we were all baptised into one Body. Endeavour to keep the unity of the Spirit in the bond of peace." He may then give the modern equivalent of the kiss of peace practised in earlier days of the Church by saying, "The peace of the Lord be always with you", to which the people reply, "And with thy spirit." In the Church of South India the spirit of this fellowship in Christ is retained in the whole congregation grasping each others' hands. Again in Series 2, before the consecrated bread is broken in pieces the following may be said, "The cup of blessing which we bless, is it not a sharing of the Blood of Christ? The bread which we break, is it not a sharing of the Body of Christ? We being many are one bread, one Body, for we all partake of the one bread." Yet again, in the prayer offered after all have received the bread and wine the minister prays that all may be kept "in the Body of thy Son, which is the blessed company of all faithful people" and that they may "continue as living members of that holy fellowship".

The name *Eucharist* has long been associated with a particular brand of churchmanship. This is a pity, for the Greek word from which it comes, *eucharistia*, means simply 'thanksgiving' and is used in 1 Corinthians 14:16 and 1 Timothy 2:1, though not in the formal sense of 'The

Eucharist'. Thanksgiving is an important element in the Communion service. How can it be otherwise? In the Sacrament we are taken to the heart of the Christian Gospel. We recall what God in Christ has done for us. We are reminded in Word and Sacrament that Christ's Body was broken and Christ's Blood was shed for us. We are exhorted to receive the Body and Blood of Christ and to feed on Him in our hearts "by faith with thanksgiving". It seems altogether appropriate, therefore, that Series 2 heads the prayer of consecration, "The Thanksgiving". As he begins it the priest says, "It is very meet, right, and our bounden duty, that we should at all times, and in all places, give thanks unto thee, O Lord."

Somewhat surprisingly the title *The Breaking of Bread* is not very popular today. The exception is with the Plymouth Brethren, who provide a morning "Breaking of Bread" for believers and a Gospel service in the evenings for evangelistic outreach. A glance at Acts 2:42 and 20:7 soon reveals that Breaking of Bread was a popular name for Communion in Apostolic days. This title helps to take some of the formality out of the service and reminds us that the sacramental acts are in essence simple, though profound.

The name *Mass* seems to have come into popular use in medieval times. It is derived from the conclusion of the Roman Mass, *Ita missa est*, a command which some modern translators render, "Get out!" It is a reminder that, having received Christ, the communicant must now share Christ. He must witness in the world for which Christ died. This emphasis on getting out into the world to witness is wonderfully emphasised in the Series 2 service, for after the brief prayer which follows the reception of the Sacrament, there are the simple versicles and responses,

> The Lord be with you.
> And with thy spirit.
> Go forth in peace.
> Thanks be to God.

The word 'Mass' is neutral, but like 'Eucharist' it has come to be associated with a particular form of churchmanship. Both words are in common use among Roman Catholics and Anglo-Catholics. Christians of other persuasions tend to ignore 'Mass' because of its doctrinal overtones.

The most popular name among members of the Church of England remains *Holy Communion*, a title derived from 1 Corinthians 10: 16–17. It reminds communicants that they have come to feed on Christ and thus enjoy fellowship with Him at the deepest possible level. This is what we mean when we pray, "Grant us, therefore, gracious Lord, so to eat the Flesh of thy dear Son Jesus Christ, and to drink His Blood, that we may evermore dwell in him, and he in us". Then, as we prepare to receive the bread and the wine, we are exhorted to "Draw near with faith: receive the Body of our Lord Jesus Christ, which was given for you, and his Blood, which was shed for you; and feed on him in your heart by faith with thanksgiving."

FEEDING ON CHRIST

"Feeding on Christ" is a thoroughly Biblical concept, but like another, "being washed in Christ's blood", it can be stated unwisely so as to cause offence. The chief passage behind it is John 6:53–56, where Jesus says, "In truth, in very truth I tell you, unless you eat the flesh of the Son of Man and drink his blood you can have no life in you. Whoever eats my flesh and drinks my blood possesses eternal life, and I will raise him up on the last day. My flesh is real food; my blood is real drink. Whoever eats my flesh and drinks my blood dwells continually in me and I dwell in him."

From the first there were some who understood Christ's words in a materialistic sense and took offence, despite the fact that Jesus warned them not to do so. "The spirit alone gives life; the flesh is of no avail; the words which I have spoken to you are both spirit and life" (John 6:63). To ignore this Christ-given clue to the interpretation of John 6:53–56 is to encourage a magical and superstitious view of the sacrament.

It is no accident that these verses are part of the long

discourse following Christ's feeding of the five thousand. Earlier He had said, "I am the bread of life. Whoever comes to me shall never be hungry, and whoever believes in me shall never be thirsty" (6:35). Just as ordinary bread satisfies physical hunger, so Christ, the Bread of Life, satisfies spiritual hunger. This is the context in which we must interpret Christ's words about eating His flesh and drinking His blood. First we must acknowledge that at the deepest levels of our personalities we have a spiritual need which He alone can meet. That need is to be cleansed from sin and given new life. When Christ died on the Cross, He offered Himself for us, in order that this need might be met. Therefore, to eat His flesh and to drink His blood means to come to Him in penitence and faith and claim for ourselves what He died to give us. "There is no magical participation by the believer in the physical flesh of Jesus, but an ever-fresh appropriation of the spiritual benefits of His passion" (Tasker's Tyndale Commentary *St. John*, p. 96). Augustine stated it simply with the words, "Believe and thou hast eaten."

"Eating Christ's body" and "drinking Christ's blood", understood in this spiritual sense (the only way in which I believe we may legitimately interpret it), is not something we can confine to the reception of the bread and the wine at Holy Communion. Anyone who has truly turned to Christ, who has accepted in faith what Christ did for him on the Cross, has "eaten Christ's body" and "drunk His blood". We cannot exclude Christian children, as yet unable to receive the Sacrament, or converted adults prevented from receiving it for one reason or another. There are thousands of members of the Salvation Army, for example, who have never received the Sacrament but he would be a very bigoted man who claimed that none of them knew what it was to "feed on Christ".

On the other hand, Christ in His infinite wisdom ordained that His Church should observe the Sacrament of His body and blood. It is a most powerful proclamation of Christ crucified, what Augustine called a 'visible word'. As we heed this 'word', as we receive the Sacrament in faith, then spiritually we receive Christ. Hooker, the great Anglican divine, said, "The real presence of Christ's most blessed body and blood is not therefore to be sought for in the Sacrament, but in the worthy receiver of the Sacrament." So then, as we come to Communion we must look beyond the symbols to the reality they symbolise. We must look to the Christ whose body was broken and whose blood was shed *for us* and feed on Him in our hearts by faith with thanksgiving.

QUESTIONS

1. Which title do you prefer for this Sacrament, and why?
2. In what sense do we 'feed on Christ' at Holy Communion?

FURTHER READING

The Lord's Supper, A. M. Stibbs (Falcon Booklet).

18

THE COMMUNION OF SAINTS

The distinguished Scottish theologian, William Barclay, says that "the Communion of Saints" is the part of the Creed about the meaning of which people are most vague. We have used the words 'communion' and 'saints' earlier in this book. To understand "the Communion of Saints" we must now look at both words in some detail.

COMMUNION

Like 'fellowship', 'communion' is an English translation of words found in the Hebrew Old Testament and the Greek New Testament. The Hebrew word is *Chabar,* the root meaning of which is to bind or join together. It is used of curtains being joined together by a seam, of nations joining together in military alliances, of fishermen joining together in partnership, and of two people being united in marriage. Significantly, it is never used of the relationship between God and man, for the Old Testament writers stressed the transcendence of God and the barrier between Him and man, caused by man's sin.

The Greek word is *koinonia.* This has all the meaning of the Old Testament *chabar* and something more. The New Testament speaks of communion or fellowship between God and man because of what Christ has done. So the New Testament word means a close and intimate bond, a partnership at the deepest level, between God and man and between man and his fellow-men. It is a two-way relationship, vertical and horizontal, upwards and outwards, with God and with men.

We can see this biblical idea of fellowship being worked out in the life of Paul. Communion with God was his chief aim in life. He counted everything sheer loss, because it was all far outweighed by the gain of knowing Christ (Philippians 3:8). He said, "All I care for is to know Christ, to experience the power of his resurrection, and to share his sufferings, in growing conformity with his death" (Philippians 3:10).

At the same time, Paul did not ignore fellowship with his fellow-Christians. Indeed, his relationship with them was controlled and sanctified by his relationship with God. Because there existed a close and intimate bond between Paul and God, inevitably there existed a close and intimate bond between Paul and his fellow-believers. So, we see from the Letter to the Philippians that for Paul fellowship with his fellow-Christians involved thanksgiving for them all (1:3), prayer for them all (1:4), confidence that God would continue to work in them all (1:6), love for them all (1:7–8), and working with them all (1:5).

Perhaps the last factor needs to be stressed. Paul was conscious that the job he was doing was too big to be done alone. He was the leader, but the leader of a team all of whom had their contributions to make. As each made his contribution, as all pulled their weight, as they worked together with a common object, so the bond between them all became stronger.

We noted that the Hebrew word *chabar* means to bind or join together and that it is used of the joining of curtains by a seam, of nations in military alliances, of fishermen in partnership, and of people in marriage. It is easy to see that curtains are joined together because apart they cannot do the job required of them, that nations contract military alliances because together they are more powerful, that fishermen go into partnership because by doing so they make more of a success of the business of catching fish, and that partners unite in marriage because they believe that they cannot live without each other. It is precisely for these reasons that Christians need Christian fellowship. In the family of the Church they find it.

SAINTS

'Saint' is one of those words that has changed its meaning with the passage of time. Today when people hear the word 'saint' they may think of an unreal and other-worldly figure residing in a stained glass window, or a great Christian character of some bygone age, or even of an especially good Christian alive today. But the New Testament 'saint' was another way of describing a Christian.

We saw earlier that 'saint' and 'holy' come from the same Greek root, the basic meaning of which is 'set apart'. In the New Testament sense, therefore, all Christians are saints, for they have all been set apart from sin and consecrated to God.

THE COMMUNION OF SAINTS

We are now in a position to look at the phrase from the Creed. "The Communion of Saints" is the fellowship which all Christians share in Christ. It is a fellowship which makes the Christian Church unique. Clubs, societies, organisations succeed in uniting people from common backgrounds, with common interests, in similar circumstances. Christ unites people as different as chalk and cheese. In Him they are one in every sense of the word. All barriers (even that of time) have been broken down. This is what we mean when we sing in the Te Deum, "The glorious company of the Apostles praise Thee, the goodly fellowship of the Prophets praise Thee, the noble army of Martyrs praise Thee, the holy Church throughout all the world doth acknowledge Thee." We are simply giving expression to the unity which we enjoy with all God's people everywhere.

QUESTION

How does our belief in the Communion of Saints affect our attitude to current world problems such as hunger and racial discrimination?

19

THE FORGIVENESS OF SINS

THE NEED OF FORGIVENESS

"Man's inhumanity towards man is as common as the common cold," says one writer. "Sin is as universal as perspiration or as the growth of a man's beard." He is simply echoing the teaching of the New Testament that we are all sinners who need God's forgiveness. "All alike have sinned, and are deprived of the divine splendour," says Paul (Romans 3:23). "If we claim to be sinless, we are self-deceived and strangers to the truth. . . . If we say we have committed no sin, we make [God] out to be a liar, and then his word has no place in us," says John (1 John 1:8ff).

Such verses remind us of the fact of sin. It is a two-fold fact. First, it is a fact of our own nature. Because we are human beings, we are sinners, sinners by birth. This does not mean that as soon as we are born we are as wicked as it is possible to be, but it does mean that we have within us the potentiality for such wickedness. This is what is meant by the phrase 'original sin'. We have an inborn bias towards evil. We find it easier to do wrong than to do right. This fact of our nature becomes, secondly, a fact of our own experience. What we are by birth, we prove that we are by conduct. Therefore, because of original sin and because of actual sin we need God's forgiveness.

The popular conception of sin differs greatly from the Scriptural conception. By 'sin' the man in the street probably means such things as theft, adultery, and murder. Though the Bible certainly classifies such things as sins, these are the fruits rather than the root of sin. Sin is basically rebellion against God, choosing to go our own way rather than His. It is characterised by disobedience.

Now as we have seen (chapter 1) God is holy. He hates sin. Sin cannot exist in His presence. Sin and God are as different as chalk and cheese; therefore, if the sinner (i.e. any human being) is to be restored to fellowship with God, his sin must be forgiven, taken away. The sinner cannot do this for himself. Even if from this moment onwards he could live a perfect life, the stain of his past sin would still be there.

This need for forgiveness is illustrated in almost any Prayer Book service we care to consider. At the beginning of Morning or Evening Prayer, for example, we are exhorted to confess our manifold sins and wickedness. We then proceed to confess that we have erred and strayed from God's ways like lost sheep, that we have followed the devices and desires of our own hearts, that we have offended against God's holy laws, that we have left undone the things which we ought to have done and have done the things which we ought not to have done, and that there is no health in us. The service begins with this honest acknowledgement that we come as unworthy sinners to a holy God. Frankly we admit that we need His forgiveness.

The same emphasis is found in the Communion Service, be it 1662 or Series 2. We begin with the prayer that God will cleanse us. After each of the Ten Commandments or their short summary, we pray for God's mercy and His help to enable us to keep His law. Similarly, in the Litany; of the hundred or so petitions forty-six deal directly with sin and ask for God's mercy and forgiveness.

So those who say, "I don't go to church because I'm as good as those who do," have missed the whole point of Christianity. The Church does not claim to be the community of the perfect (though its members sometimes give the impression that they are the community of the self-righteous!). Christ's Church is the society of forgiven sinners. Jesus did not come to call those who felt that they were righteous—His message would make no sense to them—but to call sinners to repentance.

THE COST OF FORGIVENESS

Forgiveness is, in one sense, gloriously free. We do not deserve it, we cannot buy it, and we can never earn it. Like the spiritual satisfaction of which Isaiah wrote, it is "without money and without price". It is offered to us as God's gift and it is free for the taking to all who will accept it in Christ's Name.

But although it costs us nothing, it cost Christ everything. Speaking prophetically, Isaiah could say, "He was wounded for our transgressions, he was bruised for our iniquities: the chastisement of our peace was upon him; and with his stripes we are healed. All we like sheep have gone astray; we have turned everyone to his own way; and the Lord hath laid on him the iniquity of us all" (Isaiah 53:5f). That the first Christians interpreted this passage of Christ is seen in 1 Peter 2:24f, "In his own person he carried our sins to the gallows, so that we might cease to live for sin and begin to live for righteousness. By his wounds you have been healed. You were straying like sheep, but now you have turned towards the Shepherd and Guardian of your souls." A little earlier the apostle had written, "Well you know that it was no perishable stuff, like gold or silver, that bought you freedom from the empty folly of your traditional ways. The price was paid in precious blood, as it were of a lamb without mark or blemish—the blood of Christ" (1 Peter 1:18–19). Even the hymn cannot make it any clearer:

Bearing shame and scoffing rude,
In my place condemned He stood;
Sealed my pardon with His blood.

THE EXTENT OF FORGIVENESS

Christ's forgiveness covers all sin. It covers the more respectable sins like pride, hypocrisy, and self-righteousness (and a quick look at the Gospels will show us that they needed to be covered every bit as much as the others). It covers the less respectable sins like adultery, stealing, and murder. Christ's forgiveness covers all sins except one, the sin of consistently ignoring the voice of the Holy Spirit. So with great spiritual insight John could say, "In writing thus to you my purpose is that you should not commit sin," setting the highest possible target for us to aim at, but added, "But should anyone commit a sin, we have one to plead our cause with the Father, Jesus Christ, and he is just. He is himself the remedy for the defilement of our sins, not our sins only but the sins of all the world" (1 John 2:1–2). Sin may be as universal as the growth of a man's beard, but Christ's forgiveness covers him from head to foot.

THE CONDITIONS OF FORGIVENESS

We all need forgiveness. It covers all the sin of anyone who will come to God through Christ—but that does not mean that we may carelessly stroll up and claim it at our convenience. It is free, but with conditions.

Two are brought together in Acts 20:21, "Repentance before God and trust in our Lord Jesus."

Repentance was the key-note of John the Baptist's preaching in the Jordan valley. "Repent," he cried, "for the kingdom of Heaven is upon you!" (Matthew 3:2). Likewise when Jesus appeared to begin His Galilean ministry, He began to proclaim the message, "Repent; for the kingdom of Heaven is upon you" (Matthew 4:17). The implication of the word 'began' is that He continued in the same vein. So the call to repentance was a continual theme in our Lord's ministry.

Again, it was an integral part of the apostolic preaching. When Christ sent out the Twelve, they "called publicly for repentance" (Mark 6:12). When in response to Peter's great Pentecost sermon his hearers asked, "What are we to do?", the apostle replied, "Repent, and be baptised, everyone of you, in the name of Jesus the Messiah for the forgiveness of your sins" (Acts 2:37). When Paul preached to the men of Athens he warned them, "God commands mankind, all men everywhere, to repent, because he has fixed the day on which he will have the world judged'' (Acts 17:30).

But what does it mean to repent? In the Old Testament, where it appears frequently, it means to turn—to turn from sin. In the New Testament it means to change one's mind, though the context in which it appears often makes it much stronger, to undergo a complete reorientation of the whole personality, to make a right-about turn. Whereas before the person was going away from God and further into sin and destruction, now he is going away from sin and its consequences and towards God, Christ, and eternal life.

The second condition for forgiveness is faith, ''trust in our Lord Jesus'' (Acts 20:21). We shall deal with this in more detail later. For the present it is sufficient to notice that it is really the other side of repentance. If repentance is to turn *from* sin, faith is the positive side of this, to turn *to* God in Christ. It is not an emotion, though it is sometimes accompanied by emotion. It is not merely the intellectual acceptance of certain facts about God and Christ, though obviously it involves the acceptance of such facts. Primarily, it is trust in Christ as a Person and acceptance of the free gift of salvation which He has purchased by His death.

The third condition of forgiveness is one we usually ignore. It is our forgiveness of other people for the wrongs they have done to us. We pray, ''Forgive us the wrong we have done, as we have forgiven those who have wronged us'' (Matthew 6:12), ''For,'' says Jesus, ''if you forgive others the wrongs they have done, your heavenly Father will also forgive you; but if you do not forgive others, then the wrongs you have done will not be forgiven by your Father'' (Matthew 6:14f). Later Jesus shows that He intends this warning to be taken seriously by telling the Parable of the Unmerciful Servant in Matthew 18:23ff.

QUESTION

What must I do to be forgiven?

20

THE RESURRECTION OF THE BODY

For the sake of convenience for discussion, the Apostles' Creed may be divided into two parts. First it considers the Being of God; we declare our faith in God the Father who made us, in Christ His Son who redeems us, and in the Holy Spirit who sanctifies us. Secondly comes the doctrine of salvation; we declare our faith in the Holy Catholic Church, the Communion of Saints, the Forgiveness of sins, the Resurrection of the Body, and the Life Everlasting. In declaring our faith in the resurrection of the body, we are saying not only that we believe Christ rose, but that just as He rose, so one day we shall rise.

DEATH IS NOT THE END

This is one of the great truths of the Gospel; without it much of Christianity would not make sense. Unless there is a life beyond the grave, Jesus is at best a great Teacher who was rather misguided about the future. He certainly would not be a Saviour. But, of course, the belief in life beyond the grave is an essential part of New Testament Christianity. Anyone who takes the trouble to glance at the Gospels will quickly see that their plain and unmistakable message is that we shall pass from this life to another.

Our own instinct confirms the truth of this belief. Life as we know it here and now is very imperfect and incomplete. There are so many frustrations, so many problems we never solve, so many questions that remain unanswered. "At present all we see is the baffling reflection of reality; we are like men looking at a landscape in a small mirror" (1 Corinthians 13:12 Phillips). The very frustration of this life calls for another one.

The New Testament is quite clear that there is another one. "I am the resurrection and I am life," said Jesus. "If a man has faith in me, even though he die, he shall come to life; and no one who is alive and has faith in me shall ever die" (John 11:26). The most important New Testament passage on this subject is 1 Corinthians 15. After emphasising the historical fact of Christ's resurrection, Paul goes on to state that this implies our resurrection also. Christ is "the first-fruits of the harvest of the dead" (v. 20). "As in Adam all men die, so in Christ all will be brought to life" (v. 22). After dealing in some detail with the nature of the resurrection body, Paul concludes his great discourse with the triumphant words, "When our mortality has been clothed with immortality, then the saying of Scripture will come true: 'Death is swallowed up; victory is won!' 'O Death, where is your victory? O Death, where is your sting?' The sting of death is sin, and sin gains its power from the law; but, God be praised, he gives us the victory through our Lord Jesus Christ" (vv. 54–57).

Death is not the end. After death there is new life—for the Christian, perfect life. His problems will be solved, his questions will be answered, his sorrows will be gone, and the deepest longings of his heart will be fully satisfied.

It follows that Christians should never despair at death. We cannot expect them not to feel a sense of loss at the death of a loved one; they may well be completely overwhelmed with sorrow. This is quite natural, and it is no cause for shame. But in the midst of it all they will know that death is not the end and the victory that Christ won will be theirs through faith.

It also follows that Christians must never live as if this life were all. That is the non-Christian attitude. It is based on the belief that it does not matter what you believe or how you behave, where you go or what you do, for the only life is the three-score years and ten in this world. "Let us eat, drink, and be merry, for tomorrow we die." The Christian knows better. He knows that what he is now will determine where he will spend eternity. He recognises that all life is a stewardship from God and that one day he must render his account. Therefore his aim is to please God now, and in seeking to do this he gets the best out of this life and is assured of the next.

THE SURVIVAL OF PERSONALITY

The Bible is not very explicit as to what happens to the spirit after death. People have engaged in a great deal of unscriptural speculation but this is not very helpful. Spiritualists maintain that their seances prove conclusively that the spirit is immortal. Roman Catholics (and some others) believe in purgatory—an intermediate state in which the spirit is made fit for the presence of God. But what does the Bible say? Meanwhile the Christian dead, we are told, are with Christ, a state far better than anything this present world offers (Philippians 1:23), they have gone "to live with the Lord" (2 Corinthians 5:8), they "sleep in death" (1 Thessalonians 4:13), and one day "God will bring them to life with Jesus" (1 Thessalonians 4:14).

HEAVEN

Where is heaven? We speak of it as being 'up' because it is beyond the realm of time and space as we know it. It is a state of being as well as a place of existence. Heaven is where God is. Further than that we cannot go, for there is no evidence, and anything else would be speculation.

Yet the Bible does say more about the heavenly life.

It implies that Christians will be conscious individuals. We shall not be absorbed in the Godhead, like a drop disappearing in a bucket, which is what Hinduism teaches its adherents. Rather, our individual personality will develop to perfection. We shall become the kind of people that God has always intended we should be. All that is wrong in our personalities will disappear, all that is of God will be perfected. As conscious individuals we shall recognise each other. There will be a great day of reunion for those who have been separated by death.

We shall have bodies. Heavenly life is to be preceded by the great day of Resurrection. They will be new bodies, with different qualities, spiritual bodies that are suitable for life in heaven. Paul says "We shall wear the likeness of the heavenly man" (1 Corinthians 15:49). They will be incapable of disease. The suffering that is part of our lot in this life will disappear for ever. God "will wipe every tear from their eyes; there shall be an end to death, and to mourning and crying and pain; for the old order has passed away!" (Revelation 21:4).

Everything will be perfect. That is the point of much of the poetic symbolism of the Book of Revelation. There will be no sin, no sorrow, no separation. The blind Christian will be able to see, the deaf Christian will be able to hear, the dumb Christian will be able to speak, and the paralysed Christian will be able to walk. The mentally deficient will be given perfect minds. The weak will be filled with God's strength. So Paul can say, "I reckon that the sufferings we now endure bear no comparison with the splendour, as yet unrevealed, which is in store for us" (Romans 8:18).

Best of all, we shall be united with God. We shall see Him, we shall know Him, we shall love, worship, and serve Him without ceasing. Augustine said, "Thou hast made us for thyself, and our hearts are restless until they find their rest in thee." In heaven the hopes of Augustine and of all God's people will be perfectly realised. We shall know perfect peace, because we shall be perfectly united to the One who made us for Himself.

21

THE LIFE EVERLASTING

Most people associate eternal life with life beyond the grave, the after-life, heaven. There is truth in this: for eternal life will not come to its full fruition until we have passed from this life to the next and are perfectly united with God. But Jesus taught that eternal life is something we begin to experience here and now. It is a present possession for those who have faith in Him.

One of the clearest statements of this truth is John 5:24. "In very truth, anyone who gives heed to what I say and puts his trust in him who sent me has hold of eternal life, and does not come up for judgement, but has already passed from death to life." That is such a wonderful promise that if it stood alone in the New Testament we might be tempted to question its authenticity. Can it be believed? It sounds too good to be true. But it is not a solitary promise. Jesus said similar things on other occasions. He promised, "He who puts his faith in the Son has hold of eternal life, but he who disobeys the Son shall not see that life; God's wrath rests upon him" (John 3:36). He stated, "In truth, in very truth I tell you, the believer possesses eternal life" (John 6:47). In his first epistle John writes, "We for our part have crossed over from death to life; this we know, because we love our brothers" (1 John 3:14). He adds later, "The witness is this: that God has given us eternal life, and that this life is found in his Son. He who possesses the Son has life indeed; he who does not possess the Son of God has not that life" (1 John 5:11–12).

We could spend a long time thinking about this verb 'has'. It translates the Greek verb *echei* which means among other things,

1. To have in the hand—i.e. to hold.
2. To have as one's own—i.e. to possess.
3. To have as a benefit—i.e. to enjoy.
4. To have within one's self—i.e. to experience.

In the six verses quoted above this verb is used seven times. Sometimes the translators of the New English Bible render it 'has hold of' or 'possesses' and twice their rendering is simply 'has'. Applying the different shades of meaning to the verses quoted, we see that to have eternal life means to hold it in the hand, to possess it, to enjoy it, and to experience it—and to do these things now, for it is a present possession.

Can we believe it? It sounds too good to be true. But what we are asking is, "Can we believe Him?" and the Christian has only one answer to that question! Jesus Himself made the promise. Our Lord anticipates and answers our doubts in John 3:34, "He whom God sent utters the words of God." It is in this context (only two verses later) that John records the first promise of eternal life, "He who puts his faith in the Son has hold of eternal life."

The other important point to notice in this connection is that in both John 5:24 and 6:47 Jesus introduces His teaching with the words "Verily, verily" (Authorised Version) or "In very truth" (N.E.B.). These were the words Jesus used to introduce some of His most important teaching. They underline the truth of what follows. It is rather like a teacher tapping on his desk and saying to the class, "Now pay attention. Listen carefully. What I am about to tell you is vital," and then waiting for everyone's attention before proceeding. Jesus wanted us to be in no doubt about the promise He was making.

But Bible promises generally have conditions attached to them—think of some of them, and you will see that this is true. "Ask, and you will receive." The promise is "You will receive", the condition "ask". "Come to me, all whose work is hard, whose load is heavy; and I will give you relief." The promise is "I will give you relief", the condition "Come to me". So it is with the promise of eternal life here and now. "Anyone who gives heed to what I say and puts his trust in him who sent me has hold of eternal life." There are two conditions, in reality the same condition looked at from two different aspects. We must give heed to what Christ says. We must put our trust in God. From the very moment we begin to do this, we pass over from death to life.

QUESTION

How would you answer the critic who says, "It is presumptuous to say that you know you have eternal life"?

22

FAITH

We have almost reached the end of our discussion of the Apostles' Creed; there remain but the opening words to be considered—"*I believe in* God." But these words are so vital that we need to look at them in some detail. First we shall consider the personal pronoun 'I', then the verb 'believe' with its significant preposition 'in'. By doing this we shall begin to understand something of what Christians mean when they speak of 'belief', 'faith', and 'trust'.

A PERSONAL FAITH

The word 'creed' comes from the Latin '*credo*', which means 'I believe'. The only time that worshippers at Morning or Evening Prayer use this personal pronoun 'I' as distinct from the plural, 'we' or 'us', is when they join in the Apostles' Creed. This is very significant. It reminds us that faith is essentially a personal matter. When I confess my faith, I can do no more than confess *my* faith. I am not in a position to say anything concerning the faith of the person standing next to me.

The 'I' with which the Creed begins, therefore, is a challenge. Am I confessing what I do, in fact, believe, or simply reciting what the Church tells me I ought to believe? Some people become confirmed simply because their parents expect it of them. Very often the initiative comes from the parents, not from the candidates themselves. It is of the utmost importance that parents should support and encourage their children when they contemplate the important matter of Confirmation—but is even more vital that they should not push their children into Confirmation before they are ready for it—and ready for it means, first and foremost, having a personal faith. The candidate must be able to say, and mean, '*I* believe'.

All this is emphasised in the new Confirmation Service (Series 2). In the section heading 'The Decision', the bishop reminds the candidates, "Those who are to be confirmed must affirm their allegiance to Christ and their rejection of all that is evil". There follows these questions and answers.

Do you turn to Christ?
I turn to Christ.
Do you repent of your sins?
I repent of my sins.
Do you renounce evil?
I renounce evil.

Then comes 'The Profession of Faith'. The bishop says, "You have come here to be confirmed. You stand in the presence of God and his Church. You must now yourself make the Christian profession in which you were baptised." Again, there are three questions and their answers.

Do you believe and trust in God the Father who made the world?
I believe and trust in him.
Do you believe and trust in his Son Jesus Christ, who redeemed mankind?
I believe and trust in him.
Do you believe and trust in his Holy Spirit, who sanctifies the People of God?
I believe and trust in him.

Notice that six times the candidate uses the personal pronoun 'I' as he acknowledges personally that he turns to Christ, repents of sin, renounces evil, and believes and trusts in God the Father, Son, and Holy Spirit. No candidate should go forward to Confirmation until he can make these responses with absolute conviction and sincerity.

FAITH IN A PERSON

Some people speak about faith as if it were some kind of a disease. "You've either got it, or you haven't", I have been told, the implication being that if you haven't there is nothing that can be done for you. Others think of it almost as a hobby. "Some believe, and some don't, just as some enjoy paintings and some don't, some like music and some don't, and some play football and some don't." Yet others think of faith in emotional terms. It is the "nice feeling you get when you go into an old church" or "the way your heart is stirred when you hear a well-known hymn". These popular definitions of faith are far removed from the New Testament meaning of faith.

Consider three uses of the word 'believe'. You *believe* someone when you accept that what he says is true. You *believe about* someone when you accept what others tell you concerning him is true. You *believe in* someone when, believing that what he says is true and believing that what others say about him is true, you are prepared to entrust your very life to him.

Take the example of the surgeon. He diagnoses your trouble and promises that he can operate to put it right. You *believe* him, accepting that what he says is true. You go away from the hospital and talk to your friends who encourage you by telling you glowing stories of this surgeon's successes. You *believe about* the surgeon, accepting that what they say about him is true. So far you are uncommitted. The next step is the important one—believing what he says and what others say about him, you hand yourself over to him so that he may perform the operation on you. This is *believing in* the surgeon.

The Apostles' Creed asks you to affirm, "I *believe in* God . . . and *in* Jesus Christ . . . I believe *in* the Holy Ghost." This does not mean merely that you give mental assent to certain statements of Christian doctrine; it means the handing over of yourself, body, mind, and spirit, to the One of whom those doctrines speak. You *believe in* God when you allow Him to begin to do His work in you.

PART 2

CHRISTIAN LIVING

23

BELONGING TO A CHURCH

As we saw in an earlier chapter, every Christian *is* a member of the Church. The Church is the Body of Christ, the Family of God, the Fellowship of Believers, and no one with a living faith in Christ as Saviour and Lord could say, or would want to say, that he did not belong to the Church. By definition the Church is the fellowship of all true Christians.

This Church of God is universal. Local, denominational, and racial barriers have no place in it. "It transcends the barriers of race, language and colour" (*Doctrine in the Church of England*, p. 102), and even the barrier of time. Membership belongs to "all men everywhere who invoke the name of our Lord Jesus Christ" (1 Corinthians 1:2).

Now obviously we never see this universal Church 'on parade', though it would do us a world of good to try to see it like this with the eye of faith whenever we meet for an act of Christian worship. What we do see, however, is the local church, the congregation of Christians in one particular area. This local congregation is the manifestation of the one universal Church in that one place. It is the Church of God *in* London, or *in* Liverpool, or *in* any place, large or small, where there are Christian disciples. It is with this local congregation of Christians that we are concerned in this chapter.

MEMBERSHIP

Because he is a member of the Church universal, the Christian is *by right* a member of his local church. In this strict sense he does not have to join; he already belongs, though obviously when he moves to a new area he has to introduce himself to the local church. There are, however, two types of membership, nominal and active. The nominal church member does little more than to recognise his *rights* as a member and to put in an occasional Sunday appearance. The active member, on the other hand, recognises that he has *responsibilities* as well as rights, and seeks, in fellowship with his fellow-Christians, to fulfil these responsibilities. Because the whole Church's task is to worship and witness, his task is to worship and witness, and he will do this best when he is doing it with other like-minded people.

WORSHIP

Belonging to a church involves being 'on parade' every Sunday. I believe that this is a moral obligation for every Christian. It is true (as we have seen) that the individual Christian may approach God at any time, and I have advocated the habit of daily Bible reading and prayer. But this does not free the Christian from his obligation to be in church on Sundays. In actual fact, those who neglect church attendance are usually the ones who also neglect personal Bible reading and prayer.

The Christian needs to be in church every Sunday for his own sake. Without the ministry of Word and Sacrament which he will there receive, his Christian life will be in danger of withering.

The Ministry of the Word

We can, and we should, study the Bible privately. This is dealt with in our next chapter. In addition there are many insights into God's Word which we may learn from each other, and for this reason corporate Bible study groups meeting informally for discussion are of great value. By taking part in these the Christian discovers that he is being built up in the faith through fellowship with his fellow-believers. Of even greater importance, however, is the ministry of the Word from the minister especially called, trained, and ordained to fulfil this function. The Sunday sermon has come in for a great deal of criticism in recent years, and no doubt some of it is deserved. But Christians would be most unwise to discredit the sermon and its value. Where the minister of the Gospel is expounding the Scriptures faithfully the local Christians will be built up in the faith and become more effective in Christian service, for Biblical preaching is not just an intellectual exercise—it is a means of grace.

The Ministry of the Sacrament

The other chief means of grace received in public worship is the grace that comes to us in Holy Communion. When in faith we receive the bread and the wine, spiritually we receive Christ's body and blood. As the Revised Catechism puts it, "The benefits we receive are the strengthening of our union with Christ and his Church, the forgiveness of our sins, and the nourishment of ourselves for eternal life." Having received such spiritual strength, we are all the better equipped to go back into the world to serve Christ. Although we receive the bread and the wine individually, we cannot enjoy fellowship with God in splendid isolation from our fellow-Christians. As has often been said, there is no such thing as a solitary Christian. St. John deals with this point positively when he shows that because "we are being cleansed from every sin by the blood of Jesus his Son", then "we share together a common life" in Christ (1 John 1:7).

WITNESS

God's grace does not come to us only through acts of public worship, as we shall see. Nevertheless, through Word and Sacrament we do receive the strength we need to live the Christian life. In particular, these means of grace that we enjoy in fellowship with our fellow-believers equip us for the task of Christian witness. We shall deal with Christian witness from the personal point of view in a later chapter. Our concern here is with those aspects of witness that centre round the local church.

One aspect is so obvious that it is often overlooked. We witness for Christ with our feet every time we walk to church for a service. This is particularly true of those who live in the highly populated urban areas with many houses in one road. Our neighbours notice what we do and where we go, and it will not take them long to discover that every Sunday at a particular time we make our way to the church on the corner to worship God. The importance of this kind of witness should not be overlooked. Provided it is backed up by consistent Christian living, it may have far-reaching effects. In contrast, the Christian who cannot be bothered to make the effort to go to church is telling his neighbours that as far as he is concerned the worship of God does not matter.

Various other forms of corporate Christian witness take place in any live Christian body. Obviously, some of these develop quite spontaneously. Their form is determined by the particular needs and opportunities of the parish concerned. For example, we should not be surprised if the 'coffee morning' approach fails to work in a down-town area. The important thing is that members of the local church should be aware of their responsibilities to the community in which God has placed them and fully aware of their opportunities.

For some church-members this will mean house-to-house visiting, or the visiting of the sick and needy. For others, it will mean teaching in the Sunday school or leading a Bible class. Some will be required to help run parish youth organisations. Others will be needed to help produce the parish magazine, to distribute leaflets advertising special services, or to run a bookstall. Not all have the same gifts or the same interests, and our gifts and our interests often determine the form our witness will take. No matter what form it takes, however, witness is part of the church-member's responsibility. This point is made admirably at the end of the new Communion Service (Series 2) when, having offered God our souls and bodies to be a living sacrifice, we pray,

Send us out into the world
in the power of thy Spirit,
to live and work
to thy praise and glory.

24

BIBLE READING

Chapter 3 should have answered the question, "Why should we read the Bible?" God Himself took the trouble to have it written. Its subject is salvation. That being so, it is a book written by the most important Author about the most vital subject. Therefore, if we are interested in God and concerned about salvation, the Bible ought to be given first claim on our reading time.

I imagine most readers would accept this. All Christians know that they ought to read the Bible. Few, however, get down to the business of actually reading it. Why is this? Perhaps one of the basic reasons is that they do not know how to set about it. This chapter is intended to help such people. It seeks to answer the question, "How should we read the Bible?"

READ REGULARLY

Bible reading is a means of grace. Just as physical life is sustained by ordinary food, so spiritual life is sustained by spiritual food. "You are babies, new-born in God's family, and you should be crying out for unadulterated spiritual milk to make you grow" (1 Peter 2:2 Phillips). We receive part of this necessary diet through Word and Sacrament in public worship. This should be our weekly 'feast'. But we need more than this. Daily Bible reading is as important for our spiritual welfare as regular meals are for our physical fitness.

Part of the secret is to establish a definite habit. Decide on a set time each day when you can be fairly sure of remaining undisturbed. This will be fairly easy if you have a room of your own. If not, you may have to go into church or find some other suitable place. In the early days of my Christian life I found that I could best establish the habit of daily Bible reading and prayer by visiting a local church during my lunch-hour break from work.

READ SYSTEMATICALLY

During the week after I had become a Christian, I read through John's Gospel about six times. This brought me tremendous joy and the assurance that I had been accepted in Christ. Soon, however, I felt the need for a definite system of Bible reading and I was glad to link up with the Scripture Union who supplied me with a year's Bible reading on a printed card and notes to help me to understand each passage.

To follow some such definite system is essential. This ensures that we get a balanced diet. Some parts of the Bible are less interesting than others but God has something to teach us in all sixty-six books. A varied diet also helps to avoid boredom. We cannot live on cream buns every day!

READ PRAYERFULLY

The Bible is an inspired book. Its authors spoke and wrote because they were impelled to do so by the Holy Spirit. That same Spirit of God dwells in the Christian, and it is part of the Spirit's work to make the truth live. Therefore we should approach Bible reading, prayerfully. Before reading we should pray for God's guidance. Even as we read, we should be in an attitude of prayer, that is, we should expect God to speak to us through His Word, and we should *pray home* each lesson as we learn it. In this way, Bible reading becomes not just an intellectual exercise but a spiritual experience, a daily means of grace.

READ THOUGHTFULLY

God guides us as we read, but He does so through our normal

mental processes. This means that praying must be accompanied by thinking. We must apply ourselves to the passage in hand. Remembering its context, we must ask what it meant to those to whom it was first written and what it means now to us. Again, membership of the Scripture Union (or some similar body) is helpful in this respect, for Bible reading cards have a series of thought-provoking questions to help us to get to grips with the passage. Some people find it helpful to keep a notebook in which to write down the answers to these questions.

* * *

During Christ's earthly ministry there were those who were prepared to listen to Him but who refused to act upon His teaching. He said they were like fools who built their houses on the sand. James also said something on similar lines. "Be sure that you act on the message and do not merely listen; for that would be to mislead yourselves. A man who listens to the message but never acts upon it is like one who looks in a mirror at the face nature gave him. He glances at himself and goes away, and at once forgets what he looked like. But the man who looks closely into the perfect law, the law that makes us free, and who lives in its company, does not forget what he hears, but acts upon it; and that is the man who by acting will find happiness" (James 1:22–25).

QUESTION

Discuss the various types of Bible study.

25
PRAYER

As with Bible reading, many Christians pay lip-service to the importance of prayer but spend only a few moments practising it. Perhaps this is one of the main reasons we make so little impact upon people outside the Church. They see so little difference beween us and themselves. It is as we pray and read the Bible that we progress towards Christian maturity. Without prayer and Bible reading, our Christian lives remain stunted and defective.

God speaks to us through the Bible; we speak to God in prayer. It is difficult to separate the two activities, and in practice they often occur together. Therefore, much of what was said in the previous chapter about Bible reading applies equally to prayer.

WHEN SHALL I PRAY?

Though we may pray to God at any time, there is a strong probability that if we fail to fix a definite time we shall not pray at all. We need to make a habit of prayer so that it becomes as normal as a regular meal. It is a good rule to pray at the beginning of the day, before we become involved in the day's activities and again at the end of the day, before going to sleep. This will require a certain amount of self-discipline, particularly in the morning, but self-discipline is an integral part of applied Christianity

To fix a definite time for prayer does not rule out prayer

at other times. God is always listening, and we may come to Him at any time as the need arises. But this is no substitute for the more organised period of prayer at a regular time.

WHERE SHALL I PRAY?

The kind of 'emergency prayer' described in the last paragraph can be uttered at any time and in any place. We do not have to kneel down and close our eyes. It may be positively dangerous to do so! I have prayed this kind of prayer on a bicycle, at the wheel of a car, and standing on somebody's doorstep, and as a lad outside the headmaster's study! For the regular time of prayer, however, it is useful to have a quiet place to which we may retire. As suggested in the last chapter, if we have no room of our own where we may be undisturbed, a local church may be the answer. However, the important thing is not *where* we pray, but that we do it and do it regularly.

HOW SHALL I PRAY?

Private prayer is such a personal thing that it is almost impossible for one person to lay down rules for another. In any case, as we progress in prayer we find that prayer becomes much more spontaneous and the methods earlier adopted fade into the background. On the other hand, many Christians have found it helpful to be reminded of the different types of prayer by the word ACTS, standing for Adoration, Confession, Thanksgiving, and Supplication.

Adoration

In adoration we remind ourselves of what God is like and we worship Him because of it. Sometimes this aspect of prayer springs naturally from our Bible reading. Perhaps we read a passage such as Isaiah 6, and this reminds us that God is holy and merciful, and we worship Him because of it. Sometimes a hymn expresses what we want to say much better than we can say it. I have often used the hymn "My God, how wonderful Thou art" in this way. The Prayer Book helps also, especially the Gloria of the Communion Service.

Confession

When Isaiah saw something of what God was like, his own sinfulness clung to him like a burden. Then he confessed his sin and received God's cleansing. Adoration leads naturally to confession. Inevitably, when we look at God we are compelled to look at ourselves and we face up to our own shortcomings. An important part of prayer is to confess these, to repent of them, to receive cleansing for them, before getting up and going back to overcome them.

A word of warning may be necessary here, however, for some Christians become very depressed at their own sinfulness. While we remain in this life we shall fail God time and time again. We shall not know perfection this side of heaven. We shall not bring glory to God by grovelling in our own sinfulness, however, but by facing up to it in a realistic manner, confessing it, claiming God's cleansing in Christ, and relying upon the power of His spirit to enable us to do better in the future.

Thanksgiving

This is a neglected part of prayer, for we often make the mistake of thinking that prayer means only asking for things. As well as the obvious causes for thanksgiving, the great objective facts of the Gospel and how we have been led to believe them, we should make a point of saying our own personal 'thank-yous' for the way God deals with us individually.

Supplication

It is perhaps to Supplication that we most often turn. Obviously there will be our own personal needs and those of our family and friends to bring to God; then the needs of own church and parish, our country, the overseas work of the Church, and many other things. This part of our prayer life can be organised best by using a prayer list with a few selected items for each day of the week. Some churches produce their own, as do missionary societies.

HOW SHALL I WORD MY PRAYER?

Some people get very perturbed because they are not sure how to express themselves when praying to God. Though God is holy and we should approach Him with reverence, it is important to remember that when we pray we are talking to our loving heavenly Father. He is not concerned about our 'thees' and 'thous', our 'wilts' and 'shalts', but with the fact that we love Him, and trust Him, and want to talk to Him. Though it is helpful to use other people's prayers, as well as hymns and psalms, we should not neglect our own extempore prayer, and it should be our own, avoiding those high-sounding phrases and religious clichés which we would not dream of using in any other context. God does not want us to play a part, but to be natural. After all, He knows what we are really like anyway!

FURTHER READING

Prayer Secrets, Guy King (Marshall, Morgan & Scott).
Prayer, O. Hallesby (I.V.F.).
The Quiet Time (I.V.F.).
In the Secret Place (Scripture Union).

The importance of this sphere of witness cannot be exaggerated. Whilst doing your job you will come into contact with the greatest number of non-Christians. For some of them you may be the only contact they have with a committed Christian. Here is a wonderful opportunity of witnessing for Christ. You will not do this most effectively by talking about the church all the time (they will soon find that boring), or even talking much about Christ and your faith (you are there to do a job of work, not to preach) but by working to the best of your ability. People watch you and see how you work. Is your attitude to your job more Christian than theirs?

"BE READY TO ANSWER"

I have emphasised the point that we must witness for Christ by the way we live and the way we work. Actions speak louder than words. I have never forgotten the comment of an old Norfolk woman about a preacher who did not practise, "He's all say and no do." We must not overlook the fact, however, that if we are witnessing for Christ by our lives and in our work, God may eventually give us the opportunity to witness with our lips. We should not badger people about religion, but we ought to be prepared to speak when the opportunity comes.

What are we to speak about? Our church? sometimes. Morality? Perhaps. Our chief aim is to speak about Christ. If He means anything to us, then we shall want to pass on the good news. In doing this, we shall be following the advice of Peter, "Be ready at any time to give a quiet and reverent answer to any man who wants a reason for the hope that you have within you" (1 Peter 3:15 Phillips).

QUESTION

What problems for Christian witness are you likely to find in your place of employment?

FURTHER READING

Facing the Facts, W. F. Batt (I.V.F.).

27

STEWARDSHIP

The first thing to remember in any discussion of Christian stewardship is that we are not our own. We belong to God. He is creator and Redeemer. He made us and, in Christ, He bought us. It follows from this that there is not one part of our lives that we may seek to hide from His scrutiny or withhold from His Lordship. As has often been said, if He is not Lord of all, He is not Lord at all.

This is the basis of Christian stewardship. All that we are, we owe to Him. All that we have, belongs to Him. Life itself is a gift which He has entrusted to us. We must use it to God's glory. This has many practical implications. We shall concentrate on those which concern the use of our time, our talents, and our money.

TIME

Because the whole of life is a stewardship, we must not imagine that God has no further claims on our time when we have been to church once on Sunday. We belong to God, body, mind, and spirit, for twenty-four hours a day and for seven days a week, all the year round. It follows that God is just as concerned with what we do on Wednesday at 3 p.m. or on Friday at 11 p.m. as He is with what we do on Sunday at 11 a.m. or 6.30 p.m.

This does not mean that we have 'no time of our own' in the sense that all our leisure time must be taken up with what we are pleased to call 'religious pursuits' or 'church activities'. We have a responsibility to our family, and we must give time to them; we have a responsibility to ourselves, to keep ourselves mentally and physically fit, and we must give time to that. Nor does this approach exclude the use of leisure time for hobbies and other forms of relaxation.

But we must be honest with ourselves. As stewards of the time God has given us (and we must never forget that we do not know how much more of it there is) we must ask ourselves whether we are using it in the way God intended. What proportion of our time is taken up with Christian worship, with private Bible reading and prayer, with Christian witness, with service to the community? By all means let us enjoy our sport, our reading, our television and our other activities, but let us make sure they are not usurping the place which should be occupied by other things.

TALENTS

God has given all of us our talents. In some people His gifts are quite spectacular: in most they are very ordinary. But spectacular or ordinary, they have been given us not merely for our pleasure and profit, but for His glory. When they are viewed in this light the pleasure they bring to us is the greater.

The main sphere in which we are to use our talents is our daily work (though it must be conceded that there are still many forms of employment which make this almost an impossibility). In addition, we should be prepared to use our talents in the fellowship of the church and for the benefit of the local community. The stewardship of our talents, therefore, will involve asking, "What am I good at?" and "How can I use my ability for God in His Church?"

MONEY

Two of the key New Testament passages concerning giving are 2 Corinthians 8–9 and 1 Corinthians 16:2. Both should be studied carefully. From them we learn that Christian giving should be, (*a*) *Regular:* "Every Sunday each of you is to put aside and keep by him a sum" (1 Corinthians 16:2).

(*b*) *Proportionate:* "A sum in proportion to his gains" (1 Corinthians 16:2). In Old Testament days every Jew was expected to give one-tenth of his income. There is no New Testament law on the subject but many Christians feel that they cannot give less than the Jews did. Certainly, if tithing were adopted as a general principle in the Church all our financial problems would be solved very quickly. The important thing is that every Christian should make his own definite decision. As Paul says, "Each person should give as he has decided for himself; there should be no reluctance, no sense of compulsion; God loves a cheerful giver" (2 Corinthians 9:7).

(*c*) *Generous,* and even *Sacrificial:* Paul says the Macedonian Christians showed theselves "lavishly open-handed" from the "depths of their poverty" (2 Corinthians 8:2). They not only went "to the limit of their resources" but even "beyond that limit" (2 Corinthians 8:3). In this respect it needs to be remembered that what is generous for one person is mean for another, and *vice versa.* The giving of the poor widow was certainly sacrificial, though she gave less than anyone else (Mark 12:41–44). This kind of giving will come about only as we remind ourselves over and over again of what Christ gave for us. "You know how generous our Lord Jesus Christ has been: he was rich, yet for your sake he became poor, so that through his poverty you might become rich" (2 Corinthians 8:9).

* * *

Above everything else, however, Christian stewardship means not just the giving of our time, talents, and money to the Lord, but our very selves. Again the Macedonian Christians provide us with an example. "Their giving surpassed our expectations; for they gave their very selves, offering them in the first instance to the Lord" (2 Corinthians 8:5).

This was the kind of giving that Frances Havergal had in mind when she reached the climax of her great hymn with the verse,

Take my love; my Lord, I pour
At Thy feet its treasure store.
Take myself, and I will be
Ever, only, all, for Thee!

This is the meaning of Christian stewardship.

QUESTION

How much of *me* is given to the Lord?

FURTHER READING

Direct Giving and Parish Finance, D. K. Dean (Falcon Booklet).
Exodus 36.

Have faith in God,
And Know he always
Loves You,

Love Lorraine
xx
/76.

To
Steve
God bless,
Robby

To Steve
all ways
believe
in
him
all my
love
Irene
xxx
/76.

To Steve
You can do all
things with faith
Jan

To Steve.
Keep close to Jesus
Helen

To Steve
May Christ's love
be in you forever.
John